The Citizen's Official Guide to Crime Prevention

By Don E. Fletcher, Sarah Kaip, and David Sours

Edited by:
Ted E. Lawson, Thomas N. Monson, Diana Fairbanks and Nancy Moran

A Publication of Community Watch
Advantage Source, Inc.
Medford, OR

The Citizen's Official Guide to Crime Prevention
Publication of Community Watch

Library of Congress Cataloging-in-Publication Data

Fletcher, Don E.
The citizen's official guide to crime prevention / by Don E. Fletcher, Sarah Kaip,
and David Sours ; edited by Ted E. Lawson, Thomas N. Monson, and Nancy
Moran.
p. cm.
ISBN 0-9743830-4-X
1. Crime prevention. 2. Crime prevention--Citizen participation. I. Kaip, Sarah.
II. Sours, David. III. Title.

HV7431.F64 2004
364.4'3--dc22
2004012381

Advantage Source website: www.crimeprevent.com

ISBN 0-9743830-4-X

Contents

Community and Neighborhood Watch

Welcome to the Power of Community Watch

You've heard the story before. Perhaps you've even experienced it in your own neighborhood. A crime is in progress. A neighbor happens to observe something suspicious and notifies the police. Fortunately, their response is swift, and the criminal is apprehended. The best part is, word gets around among the criminals in the area: "Stay away from that neighborhood. People look out for each other over there."

These are the reasons people give for joining Community Watch:

- To look out for each other.
- To reduce crime.
- To get to know each other better.
- To provide a safe environment for their kids.
- To make their community stronger.
- To solve problems together.

Community Watch fulfills all of these needs, and more. Community Watch is a system of bringing citizens together with law enforcement, the fire department, health agencies, the schools, and other organizations to address issues and needs of mutual concern. As you will soon discover, Community Watch has a lot in common with Neighborhood Watch, but there are some important differences. Community Watch is <u>what you need it to be</u>, and therein lies its power.

The Citizen's Official Guide to Crime Prevention will show you just how you and your family can benefit from being involved in a Community Watch program. Over the past several decades, Community Watch has become vital to the development and preservation of healthy, safe neighborhoods in cities and counties all across the USA and Canada. Whether you live in a rural area, a coastal community, a multi-family dwelling in an urban neighborhood, or on a cul-de-sac in suburbia, this handbook will help you to become productively engaged with a program that will make a difference to you and your neighborhood.

The first thing you need is a clear idea of what you can expect from Community Watch. For most people, concern about crime is a key motivator for joining a block group, but it isn't the sole motivator. Many issues are addressed through

Community Watch programs, and many needs are served. Among the issues that these programs have addressed are drug abuse prevention, first aid, disaster preparedness, city and county planning, and fire prevention and safety. Among the needs being served are the desire for social interaction, the desire to give back to the community and to help others, and the need to be part of a team (of something larger than yourself).

What do you need? Chances are good that Community Watch can help you get it. In a world of uncertainty marked by terrorist acts and limited local and state budgets, Community Watch provides an infrastructure for citizens to work together with law enforcement, social services, and a variety of business and agency partners—an infrastructure that can help find local solutions to pressing problems. In the process, many people find friendship, caring communities, and deep fulfillment.

What Community Watch Is

Community Watch is primarily a crime prevention program that:

- Teaches citizens techniques to reduce the risk of being victimized at home and in public.
- Trains citizens on the importance of recognizing suspicious activities and how to report them.
- Teaches participants how to make their homes more secure and properly identify their property.
- Allows neighbors to get to know each other and their routines so that any out of place activity can be reported and investigated.
- Creates a cohesive body of concerned citizens that can address other issues that concern the entire community.
- Encourages individual citizens and neighborhoods to work together with governmental, non-profit and business partners in an agile grassroots organization where individual initiative makes a difference and positive change is the norm.

What Community Watch Is Not

- A vigilante force working outside the normal procedures of law enforcement.
- A program designed for participants to take personal risks to prevent crime.
- A 100% guarantee that crime will not occur in your neighborhood.
- A panacea or cure-all for a community's problems.
- An organization that depends on the government for its existence.
- Something that "someone else does, but not me."

History of Community Watch

The foundation for today's Community Watch programs was laid more than 170 years ago by Sir Robert Peel, an English statesman (and the namesake of the "Bobbies," London's famous neighborhood police officers). Back in 1829, Sir Robert set forth the mission of the London Police Department: "To maintain, at all times, a relationship with the public that gives reality to the historic tradition that the police are the public and that the public are the police, the police being only the members of the public that are paid to give full time attention to duties which are incumbent on every citizen, in the interest of community welfare and existence."

In the United States, the modern concept of police-civilian collaboration really started to take hold in 1972. That's when the National Sheriff's Association developed a model program that became widely known as Neighborhood Watch. The NSA program was a response to an alarming increase in burglaries reported by law enforcement agencies across the country.

The increase was the result of several trends affecting America. Citizens were increasingly mobile. Work, school and home life were faster paced. In accelerating numbers, wives joined husbands in the workforce. Neighborhoods were deserted during the day. In turn, neighbors lacked the time to get acquainted, and they no longer looked out for each other's property. People kept to themselves. The unity and cohesion of the traditional neighborhood gradually deteriorated.

Do you think any of this escaped the attention of criminals? You can be sure it didn't! And they began taking advantage of the situation by quietly moving in and out of neighborhoods, arousing little notice until it was too late.

Until that time, America's law enforcement agencies were basically alone in fighting crime. They tended to be reactive, responding after the crime, with little emphasis on prevention. There were a few exceptions, communities where police actively encouraged their constituents to observe and report suspicious activities. Anecdotal evidence suggested that such citizen involvement had helped reduce the number of burglaries. The objective of the Neighborhood Watch program was to encourage greater citizen participation in crime prevention.

The initiative gained rapid acceptance. Numerous communities adopted and implemented Neighborhood Watch. The burglary rate decreased by as much as 75 percent. Communities reported reductions in other crimes as well.

What explains this phenomenal success? Most likely, it's because people wanted to assume a more active role in making their communities safe. It was impractical to place a law enforcement officer in each neighborhood, but it was very practical to utilize the people who lived there. Residents within a neighborhood know who belongs there and who doesn't and what activity is suspicious. Or at least they can *learn* what's normal by becoming more observant. Neighborhood Watch programs worked because citizens began *working with*, instead of *relying on*, law enforcement to combat crime in the community.

Over three decades later, Neighborhood Watch is prominent in many American communities. However, the usual model of starting crime watches block-by-block has limitations. Neighborhood Watch is usually driven by law enforcement personnel and their priorities. Police and sheriff's department representatives often complain that "no one gets involved" and that motivating volunteers is a major challenge.

What the Neighborhood Watch model often misses is that what's on the mind of the police isn't foremost in the minds of the people they serve. On numerous occasions we've heard from community service officers who had announced a Neighborhood Watch meeting only to have no one show up.

Why do you suppose people didn't show up? They didn't show up because they didn't have the same urgency about preventing crime that the police department had. Had those community service officers surveyed the residents and discussed their concerns with them, something very different might have happened. They might have identified a strong concern about drivers speeding through the area, or about fire safety following a recent blaze in which a child died. Either issue could have provided the basis for starting a successful block group.

Meanwhile, because they are often dependent on the sheriff's or police department, some previously successful Neighborhood Watch programs have run aground because of budget cuts, changing political priorities, and officer rotations. The term "officer rotation" refers to the practice of rotating police personnel to new assignments, usually every two years. Therefore, the officer in charge of crime prevention or community services often learns the ropes of the position just in time to be moved to an unrelated assignment.

Moral: Over-dependence on police management and the lack of a significant civilian component in the organizing structure can jeopardize the continuity of the program.

Enter Community Watch! In early 1990, Crime Prevention Resources began research to find the most effective model of a community-driven program that promoted public safety and citizen involvement. The most successful and enduring programs appeared to have a significant civilian component in their organizing structures. The best models went beyond Neighborhood Watch; they were civilian-driven with substantial consultation and coordination with police as well as other community organizations. They also had a broader mission beyond crime watch. These programs had a citizen infrastructure that made them conducive to addressing a wide variety of issues from health and safety to taxes and littering. They were also less vulnerable to changes at the police department or sheriff's office.

The result, published in 1992, was the *Community Watch Administration Manual*. This 530-page manual offered the best of earlier Neighborhood Watch models but stressed civilian leadership and involvement throughout the organization. Hundreds of American communities adopted the Community Watch system over the following decade. The production of video programs to reinforce what was in the manual helped these communities to mount a dynamic response not only to crime but other community issues.

Community Watch in the Age of Terrorism

Today, Community and Neighborhood Watch practitioners face an extraordinary new challenge. Following the terrorist attacks of September 11,

2001, President George W. Bush called on U.S. citizens to become more involved in their communities. Referring to this effort as a "National Neighborhood Watch," the President announced creation of new civilian volunteer programs called Freedom Corps and Citizen Corps. These initiatives, coordinated by the U.S. Department of Homeland Security, the U.S. Department of Justice, the National Crime Prevention Council, the National Sheriff's Association, and other organizations, were formed to encourage citizen involvement at the local level. They are intended as a complement to, rather than as a replacement for, current Community and Neighborhood Watch programs.

As with the creation of Community Watch a decade ago, these Homeland Security initiatives are just the latest evolution of a trend in American society. Whatever the issue, be it national security or local crime, the strength of our solutions depends on significant participation by the public, a public leading the way rather than following the directives of government agencies.

Today, Crime Prevention Resources continues its commitment to help you find those solutions. Community Watch, more than ever, offers far-reaching possibilities for meeting the challenges facing your neighborhood, your community, and your country.

Benefits of Community Watch

A comprehensive Community Watch program in your neighborhood, whether or not it is a high crime area, will have many rewards for you and your family.

Greater sense of well-being. Community Watch programs are known to instill a greater sense of security and well-being, and to reduce the fear of crime. They also create a greater sense of community and put the neighbor back into neighborhood. Community Watch also brings law enforcement and the community together as a team to reduce crime.

Reduced risk of crime. One of the most important benefits of a Community Watch program is that it reduces your risk of becoming a crime victim. The risk is reduced because participants are taught how to take preventive measures that substantially decrease the likelihood of becoming a crime victim. Through your Community Watch program, you will learn techniques of home security and personal safety, and how to band together with your neighbors to discourage would-be criminals from preying on residences in your area. Law enforcement agencies report that not only does Community Watch reduce the risk of your home being burglarized, it also leads to a decrease in vandalism, personal assault, fraud, and other crimes.

More active neighbors. You and your neighbors will become much better prepared to respond to suspicious activity. Common sense tells us that we should be attentive to unusual activity in our neighborhoods. But when was the last time you stopped what you were doing and really observed the comings and goings on your block? Do you know what car should be parked in front of your neighbor's house, three doors up? If you saw an unfamiliar service truck in your neighbor's driveway, would you think twice about it? Countless crimes have been committed even as neighbors watched. Part of the Community Watch program is training on how to report suspicious activities occurring in your neighborhood and what information law enforcement officers need.

Better informed neighbors. Yet another benefit of Community Watch is that you will gain greater access to information about criminal activity. Community Watch programs are designed to keep participants informed about local crime trends so they will be better prepared to spot criminal activity and stop it in their own neighborhoods.

Community Watch signs. By becoming active in a Community Watch program, your neighborhood may receive a Community Watch sign to post in your neighborhood. Criminals know that if a neighborhood has erected a Community Watch sign, that neighborhood is not an easy target. Community members have taken the necessary steps to deter crime in their neighborhood and these steps are probably being observed. Convicted burglars have reported avoiding neighborhoods that have Community Watch signs posted.

Knowing your neighbors. Community Watch promotes getting to know your neighbors and their regular patterns so that each of you will be able to report any activity that doesn't fit with each other's regular schedule. This means that when you're away, you can feel more secure about your property. This also instills more sense of Community and puts the neighbor back into neighborhood.

Less fear. Community Watch increases the number of arrests and convictions by serving as a network for law enforcement and the community to communicate effectively about crime activities in their community. This leads to a reduction in the fear of crime and makes your neighborhood more livable.

Infrastructure for creating positive change. Once crime has been addressed and the fear of crime has been reduced, Community Watch participants can move on to address other issues that concern the community. Such issues are fire prevention, first aid, city or county planning, or disaster preparedness—whatever your group wishes to address.

Responsibilities in Community Watch

The Community Watch system includes a Steering Committee of leaders from the community, a Program Coordinator, and, depending on the size of your community, District Coordinators. These people serve as a management team that guides the overall direction of the program with input from you.

At the block level, the two roles you need to be most aware of are your own and the Block Captain's.

The Block Captain. The Block Captain's responsibility is one area, usually a street block, generally between 8 and 10 houses facing each other. Small blocks are easier to manage and make it more likely that the neighbors will get acquainted. In many urban settings with multi-family housing, the "block" is actually the floor of an apartment building. In rural settings, it may be a handful of farms and ranches relatively near each other. In a business district, it could be one side of a municipal street or a row of stores in a strip mall. The definition of the area of responsibility may differ, but the actual duties of the Block Captain are the same.

Ideally, the position of Block Captain should be a shared responsibility between two people or co-captains. This is done so that if one individual cannot be present for training, is out of town for a period of time, or just needs assistance, the job will still get done. It also helps neighbors to learn to work together as a team and become better acquainted, thereby promoting more of a sense of community.

The Block Captains' responsibilities include:

1. Distributing information, such as a quarterly newsletter or update material they receive from the District or Program Coordinator.

2. Keeping the block map updated, with current names, addresses and phone numbers.

3. Keeping track of all persons living in each house, their profession, work phone number, etc., and any peculiarities of those individuals such as medical problems.

4. Coordinating all activities for the block, such as block meetings, block parties, etc. (like a "social director").

5. Ensuring that any incident has been reported to 911 and beginning to make phone calls on a phone tree to others on that block.

6. Greeting new neighbors that move into the neighborhood, educating them about the Community Watch program in the neighborhood, and providing them with the start-up package (this handbook, for example).

7. Participating in the training programs conducted for Block Captains by the District or Program Coordinator.

8. Relaying messages received from the crime alert system if used by local law enforcement.

9. Serving as a liaison between the District or Program Coordinator (or Administrator as the case may be) and participants in the watch program.

10. Assigning work, if necessary, such as: clerical duties, raising money to purchase signs or supplies, conducting vacation house checks, elderly house checks, and patrols.

11. Informing the District or Program Coordinator if the Block Captain cannot continue, and having the group meet to elect a replacement.

12. Ensuring that the District or Program Coordinator has the Block Captain's phone numbers at home and at work.

Your role. Residents who join the block group do so with an understanding that they must share in the responsibilities of an active, effective group. Following are the main duties of individual block group members.

1. Complete the Citizen's Crime Survey (see appendix). If you haven't already done so, please complete this survey and return it to the Block Captain prior to the initial meeting. This survey provides useful information that assists local crime prevention efforts. Your help is greatly needed and appreciated.

2. Learn your neighbors' names and be able to recognize them and their vehicles.

3. Keep personal copies of the block map, block profile sheet and telephone tree in an easily accessible place and update them.

4. Attend block group meetings regularly.

5. Conduct a home security survey of your home (see appendix for forms), and implement appropriate security measures.

6. Mark and inventory all property using the guidelines suggested in Operation Identification (see page 56).

7. Keep an eye on your neighbors' homes and report any suspicious activities to local law enforcement and neighbors.

8. Write down a description of any suspicious looking persons or vehicles and report them to your local law enforcement agency.

9. Set a good example for neighborhood children. For example, teach them crime prevention principles and show respect for law enforcement.

10. Don't risk personal injury or harm to your family by trying to make an arrest or otherwise endangering yourself. It's more important to have a good witness.

11. When planning an out-of-town trip, stop your mail and newspapers or have them picked up by a reliable friend. Notify the Block Captain and your neighbors that you are going away, and arrange to have your house watched.

Knowing Your Neighborhood

Why should you know your neighborhood? Because getting to know your neighbors, their families, their habits, the cars they drive, their phone numbers both at home and at work, any medical problems they may have, and what kind of pets they may have is probably one of the most important aspects of a successful Community Watch Program.

Knowing these aspects of your neighbors' lives will allow you to respond accurately and quickly to any emergency situation, and may thereby prevent a crime or save a life. The Community Watch system offers a variety of tools to help support you in your efforts. Your Block Captain will go over them with you, but following is a brief description of each.

Family data sheet. Share as much information as you can with your neighbors so they can recognize when something suspicious is occurring at your home. This can be accomplished by using the family data sheet. This sheet is designed to list all members of the family, their ages, telephone numbers, emergency contacts, any medical problems, family vehicles and pets, and any other information that may be helpful to emergency responders.

The block map. The block map gives you a visual perspective of your block. It's an easy reference guide to who lives on your block and can be used to explain the layout of your block when reporting an emergency situation to 911 or a law enforcement dispatcher.

The Block Captain will complete a map for your block and distribute it to all participants after the start-up meeting. For each participating property, the block map includes information such as: house color, address, name of resident(s), telephone number, street names and numbers, and a directional compass.

When the Block Captain gives you your copy of the block map, keep it in a place that's easily accessible to the family, yet safe from strangers.

The block profile sheet. This is a more detailed record of your block's composition. It includes information such as work schedules, emergency phone numbers, types of vehicles, and health information. It also identifies special knowledge and skills of block participants that could be potentially useful. The block profile sheet should be kept with the block map.

Telephone tree. This sheet is designed so that each home in the block group will be contacted should any suspicious activity be reported. It can also be used in other cases of emergency, or when general information needs to be communicated in a timely manner to the entire group.

The telephone tree provides a way to quickly communicate with every participant in the watch program. Each person on the sheet is designated to call homes until all homes have been notified as to what is happening. When the Block Captain distributes copies of the telephone tree, you will probably receive an assignment of one or two homes to call. Keep calling the homes until the contacts are successful or the emergency is over.

Following are some general guidelines for using the telephone tree. Your Block Captain will train you on the specifics you need to become familiar with.

1. If you're in an emergency situation, call 911 first and report what is occurring. If it is not an emergency or you have already called 911, then contact the person at the top of the list. (This should be the Block Captain or Co-Captain.)

2. It is the Block Captain's responsibility to ask the initial caller if he or she has contacted 911 before calling the others on the telephone tree.

3. When someone on the telephone tree contacts you, write the message down. Read it back to the caller to verify that you got it down correctly. That way you will pass along a consistent message.

4. Start calling the household(s) directly under you. If you are unable to reach those directly below you, contact the homes next in line. Continue calling those homes that weren't contacted until they are reached.

5. The homes at the bottom of the tree are to call the individual at the top to indicate they have received the message. This closes the loop of communication.

6. Note: It's a good idea to practice calling on the telephone tree to work out any glitches in the procedure.

Your Block Group

Early meetings of your block group may emphasize crime prevention training. However, meeting together on a regular basis allows you and your neighbors to receive training on other topics as well. Some block groups hear presentations on first aid, others on disaster preparedness, and still others on child safety, fire prevention, and health issues. It all depends on what you and your neighbors want. Be imaginative! You'll get more results on your block, and you and your neighbors will have more fun and become better acquainted if you're tackling topics you really care about. Your Community Watch management team has access to resources and training opportunities. Let your Block Captain know if there are particular topics of interest to you.

Now about those signs.... Block group members usually ask this question right off the bat: "Where do we get one of those Community Watch signs?"

Having a Community Watch sign without an active block group becomes pretty ineffective once criminals realize the group isn't doing anything. For that reason, many communities have guidelines for issuing as well as keeping block signs. Stand warned that if your block group becomes inactive, you could have your sign removed!

If you want a sign in your block, you will need to find out what the requirements are for your community. Your Block Captain probably has already investigated this, but if you haven't heard anything about it yet, bring it up at your next meeting.

National Night Out. One of the biggest events of the year for many block groups is held the first Tuesday in August. It's called National Night Out. First organized in 1984, NNO participation in recent years has exceeded 30 million Americans and Canadians in nearly 10,000 urban and rural communities. If you really want to sink your teeth into a project, this might be the one. Ask your Block Captain about participating in the next event. For further information, contact the National Organization of Town Watch at 1-800-NITEOUT (648-3688). Their website is www.natw.org.

What are you waiting for? Pitch in! If you've read this far, you must have a pretty strong interest in Community Watch. You have many opportunities to become involved, to get to know your neighbors better, and to make your block group a success. Here are just a few ideas:

- Volunteer to organize a block meeting or a sign-posting party.
- Help recruit additional neighbors for the group.
- Write for the Community Watch newsletter.
- Create an Internet homepage for your group.
- Organize a group purchase of emergency supplies for your block.
- Plan a block party.
- Organize a neighborhood car pool.
- Offer a training session on landscaping.
- Organize a neighborhood art fair, raffle, progressive dinner, or garage sale.

Whether you joined the block group for social reasons, to learn about crime prevention, or to make a contribution to the community; there's no shortage of projects and activities to help you fulfill your objective. Let your Block Captain know what you want out of the experience. As someone once remarked, "Action creates enthusiasm." Get active!

Future Leaders Wanted

We call this program Community Watch for a reason. It works only when individuals in the community decide they want to make a difference. It works only when individuals decide they are willing to assume the responsibility and challenges of leadership.

If you are interested in leadership opportunities available through the Community Watch program, tell your Block Captain that you'd like to meet the Program or District Coordinator. Find out where the needs are, and make yourself available for a fantastic personal growth experience!

Working With Law Enforcement

Identifying and Reporting Suspicious Activities

Suspicious activity is any event that is out of the ordinary or should not be occurring. Knowing your neighbors, their habits, and the composition of their households will make it easier to recognize and report any suspicious activities occurring in your neighborhood.

When reporting suspicious activity, utilize the 911 emergency system (where available) or dial your local law enforcement agency direct. Keep the phone number of your local law enforcement agency near your phone in either case. Use the Suspicious Activity/Crime Report Sheet (located in the back of this handbook) to help you provide an accurate description of what happened.

Using the 911 emergency system. The following instructions apply to the 911 emergency system, but they are generally applicable in other reporting systems as well. Your Block Captain will provide you with training on the proper procedures.

The first thing you need to remember is that there are three different types of emergencies: Police, Fire, and Medical. You may be reporting any one of these as a result of your Community Watch program. When contacting 911, follow these steps:

1. State clearly what kind of assistance you need: Police, Fire, or Medical.

2. Stay on the phone and answer all questions. Do not hang up until the dispatcher tells you to! Follow the directions of the dispatcher; he or she is trained for emergency situations and will guide you through the entire process.

3. Give your specific location. Use your block map to give a neighbor's address if necessary.

4. Be sure to remain calm and to speak clearly. What the dispatcher may ask you:

- Your name, address, and phone number
- What is happening
- If it is a crime, he or she may ask for:
  o A description of the suspect or suspect's vehicle
  o The direction he or she is heading
  o The vehicle's license number

Keep the block map close by to give exact addresses and directions.

You should know that emergency calls are prioritized according to the degree that persons or property are being threatened. A crime in progress receives a quicker response than one that was committed in the past. Therefore, responding quickly and accurately is important. A large number of arrests are made as a result of information that was provided by citizens. The apprehension of one criminal, especially a burglar, may be the key to other crimes already committed and will definitely reduce any future crimes. Others in your community will greatly appreciate your efforts.

The time it takes to respond to a crime in progress is a determining factor in the apprehension of a criminal. A delay by a couple of minutes in reporting a crime greatly reduces law enforcement effectiveness. Commit to calling in all suspicious activity without delay. Better to call in a few mistakes than to have one person on your watch become the victim of a crime!

Identifying and Reporting Possible Terrorist Activities

- Be aware of conspicuous or unusual behavior.
- Have you overheard threatening or suspicious remarks?
- Is that an unattended backpack or could it be a bomb?
- Do you rent or sell property and have reason to be suspicious about any tenants?
- Have you sold a vehicle recently and are suspicious about the purchasers?
- As a rental clerk, have you rented a truck or moving van to anyone you find suspicious?
- Have you seen any suspicious packages or vehicles? Unattended vehicles?
- As a hotel desk clerk, have you rented a room to anyone you find suspicious?
- Do cleaning personnel, temporary staff, and other visitors to your work premises display proper security authorization?
- Are security cameras working properly?

Coping with the Threat of Terrorism

Terrorism threatens a society by instilling fear and helplessness in its citizens. It seeks to hold a society or government hostage through fear of destruction and harm. If you need special support in coping with actual terrorist acts or the threat of terrorism, please contact your Program or District Coordinator or your Block Captain and they will help you identify appropriate local assistance.

For further information on citizen involvement in the war on terrorism, you can obtain a free booklet entitled, "United For a Stronger America: Citizen's Preparedness Guide." Contact the National Crime Prevention Council, 1000 Connecticut Avenue NW, Thirteenth Floor, Washington, DC 20036-5325; Tel: 202-466-6272; www.weprevent.org. (the booklet is downloadable from the website.)

Disaster Preparedness

Family Disaster Planning

Disaster can strike quickly and without warning. It can force you to evacuate your neighborhood or confine you to your home. What would you do if basic services—water, gas, electricity or telephones—were cut off? Local officials and relief workers will be on the scene after a disaster, but they cannot reach everyone right away. In fact, there have been many cases where people went without emergency services for many hours or even days following a disaster. Experts say you and your neighbors should be fully prepared to be on your own for at least 72 hours. What follows is a plan to help you get ready to do just that.

Four Steps to Safety

Four Steps to Safety is a plan of action that you and your family can follow to prepare for an emergency. It is based on the "Family Disaster Plan" developed by the Federal Emergency Management Agency and the American Red Cross. For more information, consult these websites: www.fema.gov and www.redcross.org. At the end of this program is a reproducible Emergency Supplies List and a checklist for conducting your own Home Hazard Hunt.

1. Find out what could happen to you.
- Contact your local Red Cross chapter or emergency management office before a disaster occurs. Be prepared to take notes.
- Ask what types of disasters are most likely to happen in your area. Request information on how to prepare for each.
- Learn about your community's warning signals: what they sound like and what you should do when you hear them.
- Ask about animal care after a disaster. Animals are not allowed inside emergency shelters because of health regulations.
- Find out how to help elderly or disabled persons.
- Find out about the disaster plans at your workplace, your children's school or day care center, and other places where your family spends time.

2. Create a disaster plan.
- Meet with your family and discuss why you need to prepare for

disaster. Explain to children the dangers of fire, severe weather, and earthquakes. Plan to share responsibilities and work together as a team.

- Discuss the types of disasters that are most likely to happen. Explain what to do in each case.
- Pick two places to meet:
  - o Right outside your home in case of a sudden emergency, like a fire.
  - o Outside your neighborhood in case you can't return home. Everyone must know the address and phone number.
- Ask an out-of-state friend to be your "family contact." After a disaster, it's often easier to call long distance. Other family members should call this person and tell them where they are. Everyone must know your contact's phone number.
- Discuss what to do in an evacuation. Plan how to take care of your pets.

3. Complete this checklist.
- Post emergency telephone numbers by phones (fire, police, ambulance, etc.).
- Teach children how and when to call "911" or your local Emergency Medical Services number for emergency help.
- Show each family member how and when to turn off the utilities (water, gas, and electricity) at the main switches.
- Check if you have adequate insurance coverage.
- Get training from the fire department for family members on how to use the fire extinguisher (ABC type), and show them where it's kept.
- Install smoke detectors on each floor, especially near bedrooms.
- Conduct a home hazard (see checklist on page 58).
- Stock emergency supplies/assemble a Disaster Supplies Kit (see checklist on page 28).
- Take a Red Cross first aid and CPR class.
- Determine escape routes from your home. Find two ways out of each room.
- Find the safe places in your home for each type of disaster.

4. Practice and maintain your plan.
- Quiz your kids every six months or so.
- Conduct fire and emergency evacuations.
- Replace stored water and stored food every six months.
- Test and recharge fire extinguisher(s) according to manufacturer's instructions.
- Test smoke detectors monthly and change the batteries at least once a year.

Neighbors helping neighbors...

Working with neighbors can save lives and property. Meet with your neighbors to plan how the neighborhood could work together after a disaster until help arrives. If you're a member of a neighborhood organization, such as a home association or crime watch group, introduce disaster preparedness as a new activity. Know your neighbors' special skills (e.g., medical, technical) and consider how you could help neighbors who have special needs, such as disabled and elderly persons. Make plans for child care in case parents can't get home.

If disaster strikes...
- Remain calm and patient. Put your plan into action.
- Check for injuries.
- Give first aid and get help for seriously injured people.
- Listen to your battery-powered radio for news and instructions.

Check for damage in your home...
- Use flashlights. Do not light matches or turn on electrical switches, if you suspect damage.
- Sniff for gas leaks, starting at the water heater. If you smell gas or suspect a leak, turn off the main gas valve, open windows, and get everyone outside quickly.
- Shut off any other damaged utilities. (You will need a professional to turn gas back on.)
- Clean up spilled medicines, bleaches, gasoline, and other flammable liquids immediately.

Remember to...
- Confine or secure your pets.

- Call your family contact—do not use the telephone again unless it is a life-threatening emergency.
- Check on your neighbors, especially elderly or disabled persons.
- Make sure you have an adequate water supply in case service is cut off.
- Stay away from downed power lines.

To get copies of American Red Cross community disaster education materials, contact your local Red Cross chapter.

Disaster Supply Kit

SOURCE: American Red Cross and FEMA

There are six basics you should stock for your home: water, food, first aid supplies, clothing and bedding, tools and emergency supplies, and special items. Keep the items that you would most likely need during an evacuation in an easy-to carry container—optional items are marked with an asterisk(*). Possible containers include a large, covered trash container, a camping backpack, or a duffle bag.

Water

- Store water in plastic containers such as soft drink bottles. Avoid using containers that will decompose or break, such as milk cartons or glass bottles. A normally active person needs to drink at least two quarts of water each day. Hot environments and intense physical activity can double that amount. Children, nursing mothers, and ill people will need more.
- Store one gallon of water per person per day.
- Keep at least a three-day supply of water per person (two quarts for drinking, two quarts for each person in your household for food preparation/sanitation).

Food

- Store at least a three-day supply of non-perishable food. Select foods that require no refrigeration, preparation or cooking, and little or no water. If you must heat food, pack a can of sterno. Select food items that are compact and lightweight. Include a selection of the following foods in your Disaster Supplies Kit:
- Ready-to-eat canned meats, fruits, and vegetables
- Canned juices
- Staples (salt, sugar, pepper, spices, etc.)
- High energy foods
- Vitamins
- Food for infants
- Comfort/stress foods

First Aid Kit

Assemble a first aid kit for your home and one for each car.

- Sterile adhesive bandages in assorted sizes
- Assorted sizes of safety pins
- Cleansing agent/soap
- Latex gloves (2 pairs)
- Sunscreen
- 2-inch sterile gauze pads (4-6)
- 4-inch sterile gauze pads (4-6)
- Triangular bandages (3)
- 2-inch sterile roller bandages (3 rolls)
- 3-inch sterile roller bandages (3 rolls)
- Scissors
- Tweezers
- Needle
- Moistened towelettes
- Antiseptic
- Thermometer
- Tongue blades (2)
- Tube of petroleum jelly or other lubricant

Non-Prescription Drugs

- Aspirin or non-aspirin pain reliever
- Anti-diarrhea medication
- Antacid (for stomach upset)
- Laxative
- Activated charcoal (use if advised by the Poison Control Center)

Tools and Supplies

- Mess kits, or paper cups, plates, and plastic utensils*
- Emergency preparedness manual*
- Battery-operated radio and extra batteries*
- Flashlight and extra batteries*
- Cash or traveler's checks, change*
- Non-electric can opener, utility knife*
- Fire extinguisher: small canister ABC type
- Tube tent
- Pliers
- Tape
- Compass
- Matches in a waterproof container
- Aluminum foil
- Plastic storage containers
- Signal flare
- Paper, pencil
- Needles, thread
- Medicine dropper
- Shut-off wrench, to turn off household gas and water
- Whistle
- Plastic sheeting
- Map of the area (for locating shelters)

Sanitation

- Toilet paper, towelettes
- Soap, liquid detergent
- Feminine supplies
- Personal hygiene items

- Plastic garbage bags, ties (for personal sanitation uses)
- Plastic bucket with tight lid
- Disinfectant
- Household chlorine bleach

Clothing and Bedding

Include at least one complete change of clothing and footwear per person:
- Sturdy shoes or work boots
- Rain gear
- Blankets or sleeping bags
- Hat and gloves
- Thermal underwear
- Sunglasses

Special Items

- Remember family members with special requirements, such as infants and elderly or disabled persons

For Baby

- Formula
- Diapers
- Bottles
- Powdered milk
- Medications

For Adults

- Heart and high blood pressure medication
- Insulin
- Prescription drugs
- Denture needs
- Contact lenses and supplies
- Extra eye glasses

Entertainment

- Games and books
- Puzzles

Important Family Documents

Keep these records in a waterproof, portable container:
- Will, insurance policies, contracts deeds, stocks and bonds
- Passports, social security cards, immunization records
- Bank account numbers
- Credit card account numbers and companies
- Inventory of valuable household goods, important telephone numbers
- Family records (birth, marriage, death certificates)
- Keep items in airtight plastic bags. Change your stored water supply every six months so it stays fresh. Replace your stored food every six months. Re-think your kit and family needs at least once a year. Replace batteries, update clothes, etc.
- Ask your physician or pharmacist about storing prescription medications.

General Disaster Preparedness Materials, Children & Disasters
- "Disaster Preparedness Coloring Book" (ARC 2200, English, or ARC 2200S, Spanish) Children & Disasters ages 3-10.
- "Adventures of the Disaster Dudes" (ARC 5024) video and Presenter's Guide for use by an adult with children in grades 4-6.

To get copies of American Red Cross Community Disaster Education materials, contact your local Red Cross chapter.

Wildfire Safety

What if that beautiful home in the peaceful countryside you worked so hard for all of a sudden was threatened by fire? In the case of a wildfire, you may not have much control. However, there are a few small things you can do to improve your chances of saving your home.

Create a safe environment

The first thing to do is create space around your home. This means cutting down trees and thinning vegetation that could serve as fuel for a fire. Clear away wood debris and other materials that could also fuel a fire. Stack firewood far away from your home.

Dispose of woodstove ashes in a metal container. Ashes can burn for several days. Have your chimneys cleaned and inspected at least once a year. Clean your roofs and gutters regularly by removing all debris. Water and mow your grass often.

Make sure your driveway entrance is clearly marked and your house numbers are clearly visible. House numbers should be four inches high.

Plan for evacuation

If you need to be evacuated, you may have only minutes to get out. Have a planned emergency escape route. Also plan for any pets and livestock. Shelters will not accept pets. It will be even harder to find a location to keep livestock. Know where safety areas are around your area, such as meadows, rock outcrops, and wide roads.

Prepare the inside and outside of your house

Inside

- Shut off the gas.
- Close all windows.
- Close all doors, but do not lock them. Closing them will block the circulation of air and help prevent fire from spreading.
- Open the damper on your fireplace to help stabilize outside/inside pressure.
- Close fireplace screen.
- Turn on a light in each room to make the house more visible at night or in smoke.
- Fill bathtubs and sinks with water.
- Take down curtains.
- Move furniture away from windows and doors.

- Park car in driveway.
- Close garage doors but leave unlocked. Disconnect automatic garage door opener.

Outside

Only if you have time should you prepare the outside of your house.

- Remove combustible items from around the house, including things like outside furniture, tarp coverings, and gas canisters.
- If it's possible to close them, close the attic, eave, and basement vents.
- Close window shutters.
- Place a lawn sprinkler on your roof.

Personal Safety

Basic Personal Safety

Taking precautionary measures to keep out of harm's way does more to prevent you from becoming a victim of assault than anything else you can do. Following is an introduction to Personal Safety techniques. Your Block Captain and Program Coordinator have access to comprehensive material on this topic, so ask them about arranging a training session for your Block Group.

Avoid high-risk situations.
- Limit your exposure in parking garages, alleys and any other areas where you are uncomfortable, or where criminals can avoid detection.
- If you are driving in high crime areas, lock your doors and windows.
- When traveling, ask hotel personnel about areas to avoid while in town.

Don't be an easy mark.
Be aware of the movement characteristics of high-risk assault victims, including:
- a stride that is too long or short;
- placing the whole foot down at once instead of heel to toe; and
- body movement lacking in confidence—it seems to come from outside the body rather than from within.

Walk from your center and portray an alert, purposeful, determined and confident stride. Look ahead of you and do not become too focused on specific objects. Pay attention to what is happening on the street or area around you.

Stay in good physical condition.
- By staying fit, you will feel better about yourself, which in turn produces a more confident stride.
- This will send a signal to would-be assailants that you can take care of yourself.

Don't walk alone.
- Walking with at least one other person will reduce the chance of attack by 67%.
- Walking with two or more people can reduce it up to 90%.
- Walking with a large dog is also a good idea.

Walk in well-populated areas with good lighting.
- The higher the concentration of people in the area you are traveling in, the less chance you have of being attacked.
- Good lighting increases the likelihood of detection and deters assailants.

If carrying a purse, use one with a shoulder strap.
- Keep the flap side of the purse toward your body.
- If it has a zipper, keep it zipped up.

What to do during a confrontation:
- Don't panic.
- Estimate the risk of physical injury, and if possible, take control of the situation.
- Try to confuse the attacker, then run if possible.
- Yell "Fire" to get attention of nearby people.

If it's too late and the assailant has control of you, remain calm and remember:
- Make no sudden movements.
- No amount of money is worth putting your life on the line.
- Cooperate with the assailant: give him or her what he or she wants as fast as possible.
- Get a good description.
- Attempt to get away only if you are ***absolutely positive*** that your life is in danger.
- If a weapon is visible, take every threat seriously.
- If the attacker claims to have a weapon but it is not visible, you might ask to see it.
- Concentrate on the person, not the weapon.

Conclusion

Remember, each situation is different and you will have to assess the position you are in to the best of your ability. These are suggestions only; there are no foolproof ways to handle every circumstance that occurs. The methods listed above have worked for others and might work for you as well.

Sexual Assault Prevention

Introduction

Unfortunately, more than ever, rape is a problem in this country. A large number of rapes and attempted rapes go unreported each year. For the number of sexual assaults to decrease, this crime must be reported so that offenders can be stopped.

What is rape?

Rape can be defined as sexual intercourse, attempted or executed, without the victim's consent, with the use or threat of force. Rape is not only devastating to the victim, it also affects the lives of friends and relatives. When a family member, friend, neighbor, or community member has been raped, the psychological effects take a toll on everyone around them.

Myths about rape

There are a number of misconceptions about rape, including these:

Myth: Rape is a crime of passion.
Truth: Rape is a crime of violence, not passion. The attacker is hostile and uses sex as a weapon to hurt and humiliate the victim.

Myth: The rapist does not know the victim.
Truth: The rapist is not always a stranger to the victim. In 50 to 70 percent of all

reported cases, the attacker is a friend, relative, or acquaintance of the victim.
Myth: The victim invites the assault by dressing seductively.
Truth: Rape does not result because of uncontrolled passions or because someone is dressed seductively.

Myth: Only attractive females are the victims of rape.
Truth: Victims of rape can be wives, children, working women, grandmothers, mothers, students, rich, poor, and even men. There is no single type of person that is a rape victim.

Myth: Rape occurs only in high-risk situations—while walking alone at night, hitchhiking, or alone in a bar.
Truth: Rape can happen day or night in ordinary, seemingly safe places. Approximately one-third of all rapes occur in, or near, the victim's home.

Myth: It isn't rape if the sex is between friends.
Truth: If you are forced to have sex with someone, even if you know the person, it is still rape and it is still a crime. Just because you know someone doesn't mean he or she has the right to force him or herself on you.

Myth: Rapists are seedy perverts.
Truth: Generally, a rapist does not look like some sex-crazed psychopath and his (her) behavior doesn't appear to be odd or peculiar.

Tips for preventing sexual assault

At home. Here are some suggestions on what you can do to make your residence less vulnerable to a would-be rapist.

Conduct a home security survey. Your local law enforcement agency should be able to help conduct such a survey. Then follow their recommendations. (If your local agency is unable to provide this service, you can conduct your own survey using the form provided at the end of this section.)

Be sure to consider these easy and effective ways to secure your home: Install either wood or metal solid-core doors (minimum 2 inches thick). Install good locks, such as a deadbolt with a 1-inch throw rather than a chain lock. Change or re-key when you move into a new house or apartment. Ensure that the exterior is well lit, especially the entrances. Install a peephole viewer in the door. Ensure that all windows and sliding glass doors can be locked securely.

Check the identification of anyone selling something or offering to make repairs to your home. Have the ID slipped under the door. Call the company to be certain.

If you live alone, use only the first initial and last name on mailboxes and in phone directories or consider having your number unlisted.

When strangers call, stay in control of the situation. Don't say anything to make them think you live or are alone. If strangers want to use the telephone and claim to have an emergency situation, make the call for them while they wait outside. Never allow strangers to enter your home.

Never open the door for strangers. If you live in an apartment, avoid being in the laundry room or garage alone, particularly at night. When you come home, if you find a door or window open, or it appears that someone has forced entry into your home, don't go in. Find the nearest phone and call the police.

Outside. When you're on a walk, follow these guidelines. Pay attention to your surroundings and the people around you. If possible, travel with a friend. Stay in areas that are well lit. Try not to walk in the dark.

Walk on the side of the street facing traffic and walk with a confident stride. Remember, rapists look for someone who appears weak and vulnerable. Note: Walking while facing traffic is also the best way to avoid getting in a vehicle-pedestrian accident. Stay away from doorways, bushes, and alleys; rapists can use these to hide in. Walk close to the curb to avoid them and look behind you periodically.

Wear clothing that allows you freedom of movement. If being followed, get to a well-lit area where there are a number of people as quickly as possible. If a car is following you, cross the street, or turn and walk the opposite direction. If asked directions by someone in a car, reply from a distance and don't get too close to the car. If in danger, scream and run. Yell "FIRE," break a window, do whatever you have to do to attract help.

Let a family or friend know your route. If possible, carry a cell phone. Do not wear headphones or listen to music that blocks out surrounding sounds. You will never hear an attacker behind you. Do not run on isolated walking trails.

In the car. Whether you're on a trip or just doing errands, traveling by car requires its own special precautions. Keep your car in good working condition and the gas tank at least half full. Park in well lit areas and lock the doors, even if you're going to be away only for a short time. When returning to the car, have the keys ready and check the inside before getting in. Keep the doors locked when driving.

Never pick up a hitchhiker, even a female hitchhiker. If your car breaks down, put the hood up, get back inside, lock the doors, and turn on the flashers. Use flares if you have them, and attach a white cloth to the antenna. If someone stops to help, roll down the window just a crack and ask him or her to call the police or a tow truck.

If you think you are being followed, do not drive home. Drive to a police station, fire station, garage, or any public place where you can call the police. Do not leave the car unless you can do so safely. Try to get a description and license plate number of the car following you.

Avoid driving in areas where you would not want to break down. Do not stop to help another motorist that has broken down. Go to the nearest phone and call for assistance. Use caution when parking in underground and parking garages. Avoid doing so alone.

If possible, carry a cell phone or a CB radio with you. The advantage of CB radio is that there are no monthly charges. Also, high call volume can cause cell phone lines to be overloaded during an emergency.

Hitchhiking is extremely dangerous and strongly discouraged. If you have no other choice, follow these guidelines:

- Do not hitchhike alone.
- Accept rides from women, older couples or families, never from single men or groups of men.
- Find out where the driver is going before telling him or her your destination.
- Do not accept rides in cars that have electric door lock (that is, locks that the driver controls). This probably means you should stick to older vehicles.
- Be cautious of the driver's behavior. If possible, keep some form of weapon in your hand, like your keys. Pepper spray is now legal for adults in all 50 states. (However, it is illegal to take it aboard a plane.)
- Remain calm if the driver refuses to take you to your destination. Try to get him or her to stop for something to eat or drink and if possible, escape during this time.

What to do if you're attacked

Remember that if you are attacked by a rapist, nobody can tell you what you should do. Each situation is different and there are no definite answers. It will depend on you, the attacker, and the situation.

Remain calm. Always do your best to remain calm and keep your wits about you. Rationally evaluate the options available and assess the situation. The main concern must always be your safety. If you feel you might get hurt defending yourself, or if you are afraid to fight back, then don't.

The rapist is the criminal, not you. Submitting because you are afraid for your safety, or the safety of your family, does not mean you have consented. Victims who submit to rape should never feel guilty. The rapist committed the crime, not the victim.

Potential responses. There are a number of potential ways to dissuade an attacker, including:

- Calming him. Talk to him about not carrying out the attack and try to gain his confidence.
- Telling the attacker that you are pregnant or have some disease, like the HIV virus or venereal disease (V.D.).
- Telling him that your husband, boyfriend, or friend is on his way over.
- Doing something strange. Act insane, cry hysterically, throw up, or pick your nose.
- Stalling the attack. Offer to fix him or her a drink and look for an escape.

You may choose to resist physically by fighting back, screaming, using a weapon or self-defense techniques. Keep in mind that this type of active resistance may lead the rapist to become more violent. Be cautious. Being prepared before an attack occurs and knowing your options ahead of time are the best defensive moves you can take.

What to do after a rape has occurred

If you have been assaulted, call the police, a relative, friend, doctor, or rape crisis center immediately. Get help as soon as possible. The sooner the report is made to law enforcement, the higher probability the attacker will be caught. Law enforcement can also put you in touch with community services to help you deal with the attack.

Do not shower, bathe, douche, touch, or change any clothing you were wearing. Do not disturb anything where the assault took place. The police can use this physical evidence for prosecuting the criminal.

Go to a hospital and get examined by a doctor. The doctor will take care of any injuries and collect medical evidence for use in court. Ask the doctor to note any injuries received from the attack and later, to check for possible pregnancy and venereal disease.

Contact a rape crisis center to help you deal with the trauma of the attack. These highly trained individuals can help in many ways.

Prosecute the rapist. Most rapists are repeat offenders until caught. The conviction of the rapist who attacked you can save many others from the same experience you had.

If you know someone who has been raped

If someone you know has been raped, show her your support and concern. Make yourself available to spend time with her by going to dinner or a movie. She may just want someone to listen and to be with.

Many times victims will feel guilty and blame themselves. Let them know they did the right thing – whatever it was, they had to do it to survive.

Encourage the victim to prosecute the attacker. Rapists are repeat offenders and if not prosecuted, someone else will become a victim. The victim will need your encouragement and support to make it through this difficult time. Encourage her to also seek counseling.

Conclusion

There is additional training that can help you prevent or fend off a potential attack. Contact the YMCA, YWCA, community education programs, and law enforcement agencies for information about classes in your area. We can't afford to be shy or embarrassed about discussing the problem of rape. We have to educate ourselves as a community about how to prevent such attacks. We need to report them immediately when they do occur. Only by arming ourselves with this information, and then applying it, can we hope to deter these criminals and experience a reduction in the number of sexual assaults.

Travel Safety

Travel safety today is more important than ever. With all the crooks, scams, pickpockets, identity thieves, and anti-Americans scattered throughout the world, travelers need to take as many precautions as they can to stay safe.

These are some basic travel safety tips to ensure your family enjoys its next vacation.

Hotel Safety

- Ask for a room on the second to seventh floor.
- Find out if there is on-site security.
- Verify that the window and door locks are secure.
- Put valuables in the hotel safe and get a receipt.
- Be careful of exits and elevators on the way to your room. Get an escort to your room late at night or if alone.
- Be suspicious of anyone loitering anywhere in the hotel.
- Don't leave windows open.
- Count the number of doors to the fire exit and know where the extinguishers and alarms are.
- Call the desk if someone unexpected knocks at your door.
- Cancel maid service.
- Make a list of your incoming and outgoing calls, so you don't get charged for calls you didn't make.
- Dinnertime is the most popular times for burglaries.
- If someone calls saying he or she is from the front desk and needs to confirm your credit card number, do not give it out over the phone. Walk down to the desk to confirm they asked for it.

International Travel

- Do not leave your luggage unattended even for a minute.
- Do not accept packages from strangers.
- Avoid luggage tags, dress, and behaviors that may identify you as an American.

- Try to minimize the time spent in public areas at airports. Move quickly from the check-in counter to secured areas.
- Carry photocopies of all necessary documents including: health certificates signed by your MD, letters from MD about necessary prescriptions, driver's licenses, spare passport photos, birth certificates, etc. Carry these in a plastic, waterproof, zip lock bag.
- Do not put valuables in your suitcase. European countries will compensate lost luggage by weight rather than value.
- Keep in mind that you can be arrested overseas for actions that are either legal or minor infractions in the U.S.
- Always assume you are being watched.
- Find out what the favorite scams are locally.
- Try not to venture out alone. Take a buddy.
- Carry valuables in a money belt. Transfer money from your belt to your pocket in a restroom.
- Inform someone of your itinerary.
- Don't get distracted when people ask for directions, a match, or a handout. Keep moving, especially away from a fake argument or street fight.

If you plan to travel abroad, consult the U.S. State Department's Public Announcements, Travel Warnings, Consular Information Sheets, and regional travel brochures, all of which are available at the Consular Affairs Internet website at http://travel.state.gov.

Carjacking

It is nearly impossible to steal a new car these days. Sophisticated alarms and improved locking devices make it difficult for thieves to steal unoccupied cars. That is why carjacking is on the rise. According to the FBI, a carjacking occurs every 20 seconds. Carjacking occurs when a car is taken from a person by force. Most victims are affluent. Expensive vehicles are prime targets.

Carjacking occurs mostly in big cities at night. Carjackers look for intersections controlled by stoplights or signs. They also look for victims in parking garages and lots. Self-serve gas stations, car washes, ATMs, and residential driveways or streets are also popular spots for carjacking. However, it can happen anywhere, any time, to anybody.

Prevention

There are many things you can do to avoid a carjacking.
- Park in well-lit, non-secluded areas. Avoid parking near places a person can hide in or behind, such as dumpsters, large vans, or shrubbery. If you have to park in a parking garage, choose a garage that has an attendant.
- When approaching your car, have your car key in your hand. Be alert to what is going on around you, especially people walking toward you. If someone seems to be loitering near your car, keep walking until that person leaves.
- Scan around, under, and inside your vehicle before getting in.
- Lock your doors and windows when you drive. It is best if you can use air conditioning or only open windows halfway. Power locks and windows are safer than manual.
- Lock your doors and start your car as soon as you get into it. Then you can fix the mirrors and put on your seatbelt.
- Be suspicious of people who approach your car asking for directions or handing you a flyer. Never open your window more than a crack to speak to strangers.
- If you have car trouble, open your hood and then get back inside your car. Keep your doors and windows closed and locked. Ask someone to call the police for you.
- Don't stop to assist strangers if their car is broken down. Instead, you can continue driving to the nearest phone and call the police for them.
- If you are in an accident and no one is around, you don't have to get out of your car. You can hold your information up to the window. Many carjackings occur when someone "accidentally" bumps your car.
- Know your areas and your routes before you set out to go somewhere, and carry maps. You don't want to get lost in a bad neighborhood.
- Be alert when using a drive-up automated teller machine (ATM).

Scan the perimeter for people who seem to be loitering.

- Make sure you talk to your teenage drivers about what to do to prevent carjacking.

What to do if it happens to you

When stopping at a stop sign or stoplight, leave space between you and the vehicle directly in front of you. You should be able to see the pavement under the tires. This will give you enough space to escape if someone approaches your car. Try to avoid being blocked in by other vehicles.

If someone does try to carjack your vehicle while you are in it, if he is on the driver's side, turn the wheels to the left. Turn the car toward the attacker forcing him to back up. You will most likely "surprise" the attacker because he expects you to try to drive off away from him.

Keep in mind that your only weapon here is a car that weighs far more than the carjacker. Don't worry about running over his feet. Just get the car moving. He can worry about his feet.

If you are confronted by a carjacker, especially one with a weapon, do not resist. Just give up your car. Your life is worth more than a car.

Auto Theft Prevention

Auto Theft Prevention

An American falls victim to auto theft every two minutes. That's more than one million vehicles per year. Almost half are never recovered. When you consider that the majority of auto thefts are by amateurs who are just out for easy prey, this multi-billion dollar hit that Americans are taking each year is unnecessary.

Or maybe we should say silly. Because whether you fall victim to auto theft is largely up to you. Car thieves choose easy targets. Eighty percent of the time, the car doors are unlocked. Twenty percent of the time, the key is still in the ignition.

Lock your car. Take your keys. If you think this is inconvenient, it will be more inconvenient if you have to go through the process of having to report your car stolen.

Other prevention tips

- Don't leave an identification tag on your key ring.
- Don't hide an extra car key anywhere on the car.
- Park in busy, lighted areas. (Sixty percent of thefts occur at night.)
- Take everything of value with you or lock it in the trunk.
- Engrave DVDs, fancy hub caps and other accessories with traceable identification.
- Carry your registration with you, not in the car.

Special precautions while parking

Leave only an unmarked ignition key with the attendant. Avoid parking in public lots for long periods of time. Make it difficult for your vehicle to be towed away. Park with the emergency brake on and the front wheels turned sharply toward the curb. Put stick shift vehicles into forward or reverse gear and front wheel drive vehicles in "park."

Retrieval of stolen cars

If it was an amateur who stole your car, it may turn up a few blocks or a few miles away. Chances are slimmer if a professional nails you. It's probably in the "chop shop" (that's what they call dealers of stolen parts). The vehicle will be dismantled and all factory identification will be removed. The VIN (Vehicle Identification Number) is critical to identifying the car or its parts. The VIN is a federally required number that manufacturers place on the dashboard near the windshield. No doubt you're familiar with this number, but what you may not know is that it has also been etched in several hidden locations on your car.

Keep a complete description of your vehicle plus the VIN in a safe place at home so you can provide specific information to police should the occasion require it. Use an engraver to etch your initials or the VIN in additional hard to find spots. Drop business cards down window channels, into door interiors, hide return address labels, or sign your car inconspicuously in other ways to identify your property.

Consider anti-theft devices

Anti-theft devices discourage most thieves, and slow down the others. They are definitely worth your consideration. When purchasing a new car, ask about the following option:
- Steering column locks
- Alarms that activate a siren, horn, or lights when a door, trunk, or hood is opened
- Switches that interrupt the fuel or electronic systems
- Locks for tape decks, batteries, and gas tanks

There could be an insurance rate cut in store for you for purchasing these options. Ask your agent for details.

Work through your Community Watch Block Group

Talk to your Block Captain or Program Coordinator about organizing a training session at a block meeting. There have been many cases of neighbors acting together who have actually helped to put auto theft rings out of business. All it takes is implementing basic prevention steps and knowing what to look out for.

Home Security

Conducting a Home Security Survey

Home security is the process of implementing preventive measures to reduce the risk of becoming a crime victim in your home. Use the Home Security Survey in Appendix I to identify effective ways to secure your home.

Remember that most burglars are not skilled professionals. They are opportunists. They want to know you are an easy target. Do you leave doors and windows unlocked? Does your yard offer shelter from being detected? Do your neighbors watch out for your property? They are looking for unmarked items they can sell for cash. Weekdays during working hours are the most popular times for residential burglaries.

Start securing your property by using the Home Security Survey in the back of this book. Are your house numbers easily visible from the street (critical for emergency vehicles)? Does landscaping provide hiding places for intruders? Can an intruder approach your property without you knowing it? Are you making appropriate use of fences, gates, and locks? Is the property well lit? Do outbuildings present special concerns?

Then evaluate the exterior of your home. Inspect all exterior doors and windows. Doors should be solid-core wood or metal clad with a deadbolt lock with a minimum 1-inch throw. Secure strike plates in the doorframe with 2-inch screws. Hinge pins should be on the inside and non-removable. Install a wide-angle viewer or peephole in the front door. Double doors, sliding doors, and jalousie windows require special consideration (see survey for suggestions). Evaluate locks and other strategies for windows.

Proceed to the home's interior. Make use of the House Inventory Form in the back of this book. Eliminate opportunity by keeping cash to a minimum, securing valuables in a bank safe deposit box, and keeping electronic equipment out of view. Mark valuables and equipment and keep an inventory list. Keep checkbook, credit cards and important documents in locked drawers. Post emergency numbers by each phone and teach the family how to use them.

When you leave home, make your home appear occupied. Use automatic timers for lights, radio, and TV. Don't leave notes on the door explaining your absence. Never hide keys under doormats or in the mailbox. Leave keys with a trusted friend. Don't carry identification tags on your keys.

Operation Identification

Situation: Your property is stolen and you want it returned and the criminal prosecuted. Without specific information from you about the merchandise that was taken, the police may be unable to help you.

Reality: The vast majority of people reporting a theft have insufficient information to help the police positively identify the property even if it is recovered.

What is Operation Identification?

Operation Identification started in 1963 in response to a string of hub cap thefts in Monterey Park, CA. Residents were asked to engrave auto license numbers on all hub caps. Later, this expanded to homeowner property.

Operation Identification is the process of identifying personal belongings in case they are stolen. It allows them to be found and returned to their rightful owners. Burglars sell what they steal for quick cash. This makes it difficult for law enforcement to trace stolen items. Stolen items look just like hundreds of others unless there's a way to prove they belong to you. The two keys to Operation Identification are: mark your property and keep inventory records of that property.

What number should I use?

Consult with local law enforcement agencies for advice. Rural residents should check with the nearest farm bureau. The number must be acceptable for entry into the National Crime Information Center (NCIC) database. The number must not be subject to change every year, every four years, etc. The most common method is using your state driver's license number, but do not do this if your state uses your social security number as your driver's license number.

How to mark your property

Use an electric engraving pen or a diamond-tipped marking pen. Permanent markers are easy to cross out. These tools are usually available at a hardware store.

Some law enforcement agencies will loan these out. You can also use warning stickers in windows and doors that indicate your property is marked. The marks should be in a highly visible place. A thief will see that they are marked and may not even bother to steal from you. The marks should also be in an area that cannot be easily dismantled, covered, or altered.

Photographs

Take a close-up photo of any items that cannot or should not be engraved, such as jewelry. In the photo, include a 3x5 card next to the item with a description of the object. Photograph the entire room for your records. Place a ruler next to the object, or include a coin, finger, or hand in the photo to indicate the relative size of the object.

Inventory

List and describe all your valuables and marked property. Note any unique scars or scratches on the property. Note any alterations to the standard property. Note makes, models, styles, colors, cost, serial numbers, etc. Keep your inventory list and photos in a safe deposit box or home deposit box that has been rated by Underwriters Laboratory to be fire safe.

Conclusion

Remember, most theft and burglaries are crimes of opportunity. Property that has been clearly marked with owner identification is much less attractive to a thief. And why not? A thief can find plenty of other people who don't mark their property, so why should he take a chance on yours?

Home Hazard Check

Source: American Red Cross and FEMA

In a disaster, ordinary items in the home can cause injury and damage. Anything that can move, fall, break, or cause a fire is a potential hazard.

____ Repair defective electrical wiring and leaky gas connections.
____ Fasten shelves securely.
____ Place large, heavy objects on lower shelves.
____ Hang pictures and mirrors away from beds.
____ Brace overhead light fixtures.
____ Secure water heater by strapping it to wall studs.
____ Repair cracks in ceilings or foundations.
____ Store weed killers, pesticides, and flammable products away from heat.
____ Place oily polishing rags or waste in covered metal cans.
____ Clean and repair chimneys, flue pipes, vent connectors, and gas vents.

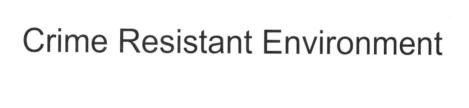

Crime Resistant Environment

Crime Prevention Through Environment Design (CPTED)

Introduction

Think of how you would go about preventing crime in your neighborhood or workplace. Ask, "What are the most obvious strategies that come to mind?"

Traditional vs. non-traditional methods of preventing crime

Traditional approaches are often referred to as "target hardening." These approaches include:

- Police cruisers
- Security guards
- Alarms
- Locks on doors, windows, equipment
- Firearms
- Barriers such as gates, tall fences, barbed wire
- Harsh lighting to illuminate areas at night
- Surveillance cameras

The advantage of these approaches is that they make your home or workplace harder to violate. The disadvantage is that they can create the feeling of a fortress, making the property less inviting to customers or visitors. Another consequence of traditional approaches is that they can actually make the property feel less safe. If you are waiting for an elevator in an office building and there are cameras all around you and a security guard, what goes through your mind? If you visit a home with bars on the windows and security warnings throughout the yard, how safe do you think that neighborhood is?

A non-traditional alternative is known as Crime Prevention Through Environmental Design (CPTED). This approach tries to capitalize on the purpose and design of the property, and identify natural alternatives to target-hardening. The place can be made more "user friendly" and still achieve greater security. You can use lighting, landscaping, building position and architecture and, last but not least, human beings, in ways that will make it a desirable place for you but undesirable from a criminal's point of view.

CPTED is a crime prevention philosophy based on the theory that proper design and effective use of the constructed environment can lead to a reduction in the fear and incidence of crime, as well as an improvement in the quality of life. CPTED concerns the use and design of space inside and outside of buildings, the positioning of buildings in relation to one another and the street, lighting, entrances, exits, and landscaping. CPTED complements other strategies of crime prevention. CPTED strategies will not be enough in every case. Sometimes you simply have to use gates, locks and cameras (for example, at a high security installation or in a parking garage).

Offenders commit crimes because they think they can get away with them. Why? Because:

- People aren't around to observe.
- Security is lax.
- Access is easy.
- No one will ask questions.
- Merchandise is readily available.

The opportunity to commit a crime is directly related to the daily routines going on in a place, including: the flow of people in and out, work patterns, distractions created by deliveries, the public, phones, and changes in patterns at night or on weekends.

The principles of CPTED can be applied to existing or proposed buildings or projects, including schools, government buildings, office buildings, churches, parks, public gathering areas, transit malls, and residential areas. CPTED is now required by many school districts, municipalities, and other buildings when new construction is planned. CPTED presents its greatest opportunity when considered at the beginning of a new project. Safety and crime prevention concerns can be factored into the architectural plans. CPTED can also be useful in modifying existing environments to make them safer.

Though many of the design solutions are intended for commercial and public projects, the principles are equally valid for homeowners. For example, placing trees and shrubs near windows provides hiding places for intruders. This is important for individual homeowners to remember as well as designers of commercial or public properties. Another example is using a brick pattern in a driveway or sidewalk to make the approach to a residence or building more appealing. It also makes the visitor (or intruder) more aware that he/she is approaching a <u>private</u> property.

Basic How-To's of CPTED

Remember three main principles: natural surveillance, natural access control, and natural territorial reinforcement.

Natural surveillance increases the likelihood of detecting a criminal without scaring good people away. The premise is that if the criminal knows he or she is likely to be observed, this will probably deter him or her.

Natural surveillance means looking for ways to let surveillance happen naturally as an outcome of doing business. For example, employees can be stationed so that they are in a position to spot unusual or suspicious behavior. Entrances and exits can be designed to make traffic highly visible.

Using natural surveillance techniques will permit you to minimize the use of cameras, security guards, or other mechanisms that can create the appearance of an unfriendly or unsafe environment.

Following are some design ideas:

1) A convenience store keeps its windows and glass doors clear of all obstructing signs. This enables a passersby to observe a robbery in progress. Keeping windows clear will create a more open, inviting appearance and bring in more customers, which will discourage criminals.

2) A mall installs a coffee kiosk at one of its less well-traveled entrances, and furnishes convenient parking nearby. This should increase customer traffic at the entrance. This, plus the presence of the coffee vendor, should deter criminal activity at the entrance. In addition, increased traffic will be good for the businesses at that end of the mall.

Natural access control means using building design, lighting, landscaping, personnel, etc. in creative ways that will encourage visitors but inhibit criminals. The purpose is not to physically stop an offender but rather to make your business look like a riskier crime target. For example:

1) A receptionist placed at the main entrance of a bank can enhance service by helping customers find the appropriate department more quickly. But the receptionist is also in a position to intervene in the

event of something unusual or disruptive. His or her presence sends up a red flag to a criminal.

2) The use of clearly marked, well-lit and attractively landscaped sidewalks can be very inviting to new customers and guide them to and from entrances and exits. By the same token, the use of low hedges, low walls, sprinkler systems, and lower intensity lighting can subtly discourage traffic into non-public areas.

3) The use of natural access techniques will permit you to utilize traditional target-hardening techniques only where they are essential – heavy security gates, metal detectors, password security, etc.

4) Following are some design ideas having to do with controlling access.

   a. Adding a second set of glass doors to an office entrance. This provides a vestibule for customers to remove or put on boots. Provides additional insulation and therefore, greater comfort indoors. Discourages the criminal by increasing the amount of time it takes to exit following a crime.

   b. Using large plate glass for an entryway, and positioning the entryway so that approaching visitors are silhouetted by natural light. Glass is aesthetically appealing and creates an open feeling. At the same time, people inside will immediately know when someone is approaching because of the silhouette effect created by sunlight.

Natural territorial reinforcement is how you convey a sense of ownership and more clearly identify when there is an intruder. The premise behind natural territorial reinforcement is that a criminal will think twice before violating a property that someone obviously cares about and looks after closely. As with male dogs, clearly marking your territory discourages violations.

Natural territorial reinforcement means using creative techniques to communicate property ownership. For example, installing decorative brick pattern in the path and driveway approaching your home will clearly delineate your property from the road and public sidewalk. Regular rotation of seasonal plants will suggest a presence on the property. Similarly, keeping lawns well groomed and doing projects on the building or house will also help to reinforce territoriality.

The use of natural territorial reinforcement will permit you to reserve traditional target-hardening techniques for where they are essential – gated entrances, trespassing signs, etc. Following are some design ideas having to do with controlling access.

1) Install a low hedge to divide a parking area from a park with an outdoor amphitheater. Trash receptacles are provided in the parking lot and the park entrance is clean and carefully groomed. The boundary created by the hedge signals entry into a quieter, more scenic area. The immaculate entry to the natural space cultivates an air of respect for the environment and provides a transition from the bustle of the parking lot to the program at the amphitheater. Litterers and vagrants will likely be deterred.

2) An alley behind a row of merchant shops is paved with cobblestones and lined with attractive lamps and flowers. Each merchant adds his own unique floral touch between the alleyway and the store entrance. A site that might ordinarily attract criminals instead invites customers because of the quiet and attractive urban environment that has been created.

Rural Crime Prevention

Rural Crime Prevention

You can decrease your vulnerability to vandalism, theft, and other crimes by conducting a careful analysis of your rural property and taking appropriate prevention measures. What follows is a sampling of strategies.

The Four Zone System

The International Society of Crime Prevention Practitioners (ISCPP) describes a four-zone method of agricultural security.

Zone 1: Boundary Security

The perimeter of your property is your first line of defense. The key prevention strategies are to post warnings, use effective gates and locks, and secure fences.

Post warning signs prominently around the perimeter to announce alarm systems, watchdogs, property identification notices, and reward programs. This sends a clear message to potential thieves that you are vigilant about protecting your property and family.

Gates are only effective if they are closed and locked! The stronger the gate, the more protection it will offer. Position gates so they will protect entrances as well as high-risk areas containing valuable equipment, crops or supplies. Gates should be mounted on sturdy corner posts and secured with heavy-duty chains and locks.

Remember that most fences are designed to keep livestock in rather than keep people out. The most secure fences are the chain link variety, with barbed wire angled out from the top. Security fence posts should be made of metal or solid wood and set in concrete.

Zone 2: Outlying Security

Outlying security refers to those areas not visible from your house or office – areas such as pastures, feedlots, remote structures, and timber stands. These are among the most difficult areas to secure. In particular, you need to evaluate your risk for theft of 1) equipment, 2) livestock, 3) grain, and 4) timber.

To reduce your risk of equipment theft, keep all non-essential tools and equipment out of these areas. If you must leave equipment in an outlying area, position it in such a way that it is not visible from a road. For example, park your tractor in a grove of trees or behind a hill, or so that the vehicle is visible from a neighbor's home. Always remove the keys from power equipment when not in use. Consider disabling the equipment by removing a distributor cap, rotor, tire, battery, or by installing a hidden power cutoff switch. Other methods of securing equipment include heavy chains and case hardened locks, lockable battery cases, and lockable gas caps. Don't forget to mark your equipment in at least two places!

To protect your livestock, mark animals clearly (brand, tattoo, ear tag, or notch) and keep records documenting sex, age, color, and unique markings of each animal. Maintain fences and look for signs of tampering. Gates and loading chutes should be chained and locked. Access roads should also be securely chained. Chutes should not be located near main roads or access points unless security measures have been implemented.

Grain should be stored within sight of your residence, if possible, or any employee's quarters, neighbor's home, the business office, or other high visibility area. Light the storage facility to increase visibility. Confetti with an ID number is sometimes used to mark the grain. Make sure any equipment that can be used to make theft easy, like augers or other loading equipment, is properly secured.

As for timber, keep a record of your most valuable trees. Mark them with permanent paint, using your own identification mark. Tap into your rural Community Watch Program. Let neighbors know when timber is to be harvested. Together you can be more aware of unexplained activity, such as chain saw noise.

Zone 3: Central Work Area

Zone 3, the center of operation, is filled with many tempting targets. Visibility is the best defense, both day and night. Landscaping should not obstruct the view from key locations such as the house. Lighting should eliminate areas of deep shadow. Keep prime targets like fuel tanks in areas visible to you but not from the road (consider underground storage). When equipment isn't in use, store it out of view in a barn or shed.

Lock your fuel tank with a case-hardened steel shackle that locks both toe and heel. Secure it at the fuel cutoff valve located at the opening of the tank (to prevent siphoning). Locking the nozzle and hose alone will not prevent theft, and may even add to your loss if the hose is cut to obtain fuel. In case of an electrically operated pump, put the control switch in a locked building or house and turn off the electricity when the fuel tank is not in use. Make it as difficult as possible for the thief to identify a target. Instead of labeling tanks, use a color code system for diesel and gasoline. Limit the amount of fuel stored at any given time in favor of re-supplying more frequently.

Zone 4: Central Storage Areas

The basic principle in Zone 4 is to make it as difficult as possible for an intruder to get in. A thief will not want to make much noise or take much time to get into your central storage areas. The more you do to keep an intruder out, the better the chances he'll stay out. Doors and windows should be well secured (see section on Home Security). Equipment and parts must be marked and inventoried (see section on Operation Identification). Some agricultural chemicals are highly sought after for the manufacture of drugs and explosives. Keep them out of view and under lock and key at all times and keep inventories to a minimum.

To prevent vehicle theft, always lock your doors. This is good practice whether you are inside or outside the vehicle. Never leave valuables visible from the outside of the vehicle. If you use a pickup, try to avoid leaving power tools or other valuables in the truck bed. Lock them in the cab when you have to be away. If you use a toolbox, secure it with a heavy padlock.

Child Safety

Child Abuse

The majority of kids pass through childhood without ever experiencing physical harm. Even so, far too many children are frightened or hurt by crime every year. Whether it is child molestation, child abduction, or bullying by a classmate, all children are vulnerable to child abuse in one form or another.

Each year, an estimated one million child abuse incidents are reported. Two thousand to five thousand children actually die due to these crimes. Abuse gets passed on from generation to generation, as abused children often grow up and victimize their families later in life. However, detecting abuse is especially difficult because the abuser is often a parent, relative, babysitter, or close family friend. Children may not recognize it, or know it is wrong when it happens. A recent complication to all this is the advent of the Internet as an environment in which total strangers can become a serious threat to children who go online.

Types of child abuse

Child abuse appears in numerous forms including:
- Sexual abuse
- Physical violence
- Emotional cruelty and deprivation
- Physical neglect

Most of these are fairly self-explanatory. Sexual abuse is of special concern because about 100,000 children are reported as sex abuse victims each year. Experts believe the actual number is much higher.

As a citizen, it is your duty to report suspected instances of any kind of child abuse by contacting the police or child welfare agency immediately. Abused children need help and treatment as soon as possible.

There is a solution

Children can be taught how to spot potential trouble, how it can be avoided, and what to do if trouble happens to them. Too few children know these things. Personal safety and crime prevention are a family effort. It's the parents' job to teach kids how to be safe.

What would your child do if:

- He or she got lost in a shopping mall?
- A nice, friendly stranger offered him or her a ride home after school?
- A bully told him or her to give the child his or her lunch money?
- A babysitter wanted to play a secret game no one would know about?
- A friend dared him or her to hitchhike?
- Someone phoned or came to the door when the child is home alone?
- He or she were sexually molested?

There are a number of precautions that children can be taught in order to avoid each of these situations. There are also times when the child is unable or unprepared to prevent a situation and can still be educated about how to handle it afterwards.

Parent-child communication is essential. For parents, the most critical child abuse prevention strategy is communicating with your children. This may be challenging, especially for working parents and parents of adolescents, but communication is essential to child abuse prevention. Educating children about strangers is a good start, but not enough. The child sexual molester, in the majority of cases, is known to the child and the child's family. That is partially why only a small number of abuse cases are reported to the police.

Teach your children what appropriate touching is. Discuss it with your child. If children are uncertain about the intentions of another person, they should know it's acceptable to say no, or to respond in a way that makes them feel safe or more comfortable. Children usually know the difference between genuine affection and when someone is trying to take advantage of them in a way that makes them feel unsafe. They should know when to pull away if someone suggests doing something that makes them feel unsafe, even if they're offered a present as a bribe.

Precautions

Discussing the dangers to children may be difficult for some adults. It's hard to believe that there are people in the world who want to harm children. Some of the precautions you teach your child will appear to contradict other values being taught to children—values like politeness and obedience.

Children need to know about potential dangers to their safety, and what to do in case of trouble. This knowledge increases confidence and self-reliance. Knowing that they can cope when you're not around will make you feel better too.

The best way to know what is happening with your child is to talk to him or her every day. Take time to really listen and observe. Find out as many details as you can about your child's activities and feelings. Encourage him or her to share concerns and problems with you.

Tell your children that their body belongs only to them and that they have the right to say no to anyone who tries to touch them. Let your children know that some adults may try to hurt children and make them do things they don't feel comfortable doing. Grown-ups often call what they're doing a secret between themselves and the child.

Teach your children that some adults may threaten them by saying that their parents may be hurt or killed if the child ever shares the secret. Point out that an adult who does something like this is doing something that is wrong. Try not to scare your children. Emphasize that the vast majority of grown-ups are deeply concerned about protecting children from harm and would never do this.

What to teach children about home

1. The first thing all children should know is their full name, address, and phone number, including area code.
2. Have them memorize your work number and a friend or family member's number as well.
3. Teach them how to make emergency phone calls from home and public phones. Practice on an unplugged phone. They should know how to dial "0" or "911" or other emergency numbers used in your area.
4. Post important phone numbers near all your home phones: police, fire department, emergency, poison control center, parents' cell and work phone number, and a neighbor's number.
5. If they are to be left at home alone, teach your children about answering the phone and not letting a stranger know they are home alone. They should say their parents can't come to the phone and take a message.
6. Make rules for having friends over or going to someone else's house when no adult is present.

7. Set up an escape plan in case of fire and practice it with your child.
8. Teach your child not to open the door for a stranger when alone at home. (The height of your child should be considered when installing a peephole in your front door.)
9. Teach your child how to work door and window locks and make sure to use them.
10. Be sure that wherever you are, your children can reach you by telephone. When they get home, have them check in with you (at work) or with a neighbor.

What to teach children about outside the home

1. Familiarize your children with the route they will travel to and from school and to friends' homes. Walk the routes with your child. Always stick to the same safe route in traveling to and from school or a friend's house.
2. Point out safe places to go in an emergency, places like a Block Home, a neighbor's house, a block parent, or an open store.
3. Point out danger spots such as wooded areas, parking lots, alleys, deserted buildings, or new construction. Prohibit playing in these areas.
4. Teach your children to stay in open, well-lit areas where people can see them.
5. Teach your children not to play alone but with friends – and to walk with them as well.
6. Show them how to walk confidently and stay alert to what's going on.
7. Role-play with your child by making up situations and rehearsing responses to them. This increases the child's ability to act rationally and calmly.
8. Let your children know the police are friends whose job is to protect them. If unable to locate a police officer, children should also know to seek out a trusted teacher, neighbor, or friend's parent when they feel scared or endangered. Teach your children to report trouble right away.
9. Teach them not to play or walk alone outside at night.
10. Be sure that a family member or other adult in charge knows where

both you and your children will be at all times, and what time you'll be home.

What to teach children about public places

1. In the case of younger children, if you are separated while shopping, teach your child to go to a store clerk or security guard and ask for help.
2. Teach your child not to go into the parking lot alone.
3. Teach children not to play or loiter in public areas such as washrooms or elevators.
4. In the case of an older child, tell him or her to wait with a friend for public transportation and to sit or stand near the driver on the bus.
5. Teach children not to display money in public and only carry money if absolutely necessary. Tell children to keep it in a pocket until it is needed.

Choosing a preschool, babysitter, or childcare center

Even though the majority of preschool and childcare centers are perfectly safe places, recent reports of child sexual abuse in these institutions have become a source of great concern to parents. Utilize the following guidelines when choosing a babysitter, preschool, or childcare center.

Check into the reputation of the caretaker. Good sources of information are state or local licensing agencies, childcare information and referral services, and other childcare community agencies. See if the caretaker is licensed or regulated in any way. Look at his or her qualifications. Have background checks made. Ask for and check references. Find out whether there have been any past complaints.

Learn as much as you can about the teachers and caregivers. Discuss them with other parents who are using or have used the program. Find out about the hiring policies and practices of the school or center. How does the organization recruit and select staff? Does it examine references? Perform background checks? Examine previous employment history before hiring decisions are made?

Make sure there is ongoing parental involvement. Learn whether the center or school welcomes and supports participation. Be sensitive to the attitude and degree of openness about parental participation. Discuss this with other parents. Talk with your child daily about how things are going and look into problems that worry you or become chronic.

Make sure you have the right to drop in and visit the program at any time. Do it periodically to ensure that the quality of care meets your standards. Take note as to how the children relate to the caretaker(s).

Let them know you want to be informed about every planned outing. Do not give the organization blanket permission to take your child off the premises.

Forbid, in writing, the release of your child to anyone without your explicit authorization. Ensure that the caregivers know who will pick up your child on any given day.

Learn about the program's philosophy and practice of discipline. Ask your child about his or her experience each day to ensure that it is consistent with what the center or caregiver told you. Ask about the use of video surveillance, and ask to see the cameras and examine the angles of view.

Signs of abuse

Encourage your children to always talk with you if someone does something confusing to them, like touching or taking a naked picture or giving them gifts. Explain that you want to be told about it. Reassure children that they will not be blamed for whatever an adult does with them.

Sometimes, a child may be too frightened or confused to talk directly about the abuse. Watch for any changes in behavior that might indicate the child has suffered a disturbing experience. A variety of physical and behavioral signals may be exhibited if some type of abuse has occurred. Any or several of these signs may be significant. Be alert for extreme changes in behavior including:

1. A loss of appetite.
2. Trouble sleeping, problems with recurrent nightmares, or disturbing sleep patterns.
3. A regression to infantile behavior such as bed-wetting, thumb-sucking, or excessive crying.
4. Torn or stained underclothing.
5. Vaginal or rectal bleeding, pain or irritation around the genital area, swollen genitals, and vaginal discharge.
6. Vaginal infections or venereal diseases.
7. A strange interest in or knowledge of sexual matters, affection being expressed in ways inappropriate for a child of that age.
8. A marked change in behavior toward a relative, neighbor, or babysitter.

The child is afraid of a particular person or shows an intense dislike of being left somewhere with someone.

9. A sudden aggressive or disruptive behavior, more withdrawn than usual, running away or delinquent behavior, failing in school.
10. Sudden appearance of bruises and scars.
11. Signs of increased anxiety or immature behavior.
12. Art work that depicts strange sexual or physical overtones.

What to do if your child has been abused

If you think your child has been abused, believe your child. Kids often make up stories, but they rarely lie about being victims of sexual assault. Your response influences how the child will react and recover from the abuse. If a child tells you about being touched or assaulted, take it seriously.

Stay calm. It is important to temper your own reaction. Remember that your perspective and acceptance of what happened are critical signals to the child. Refraining from showing your own horror about the abuse may be your greatest challenge.

Commend the child for telling you about the experience and convey your support for him or her. Many children feel guilty, as if they provoked the assault. Let your child know that he or she is not to blame, and he or she is right to tell you what happened. A child's greatest fear is that he or she is at fault and responsible for the incident(s). Alleviating this self-blame is of paramount importance.

Find out as much as you can about the incident. Use a calm, reassuring tone. Don't be angry. Explain to your child that you are concerned about what happened. Report the suspected molestation to a social services agency or the police immediately.

Locate a specialized agency that evaluates sexual abuse victims. The police know where to find a hospital, child welfare agency, or a community mental health therapy group to assist you. A child may need to be taken immediately to a doctor or an emergency room. Sometimes the child may need to be treated for venereal disease or checked for pregnancy. If your child has been abused, seek counseling from a community mental health, child welfare, or child abuse treatment center.

Find out if other parents are observing unusual behavior or physical symptoms in their children. It is imperative to take action. If nothing is done, other children will continue to be at risk. Child sexual abuse is a community interest and concern. If sexual abuse happens to your child, do not blame yourself. Unfortunately, abuse is a fact in society. Child molesters have access to children through employment and community activities.

Helpful community resources

Your community may have a Block Home or McGruff House program. This is an adult-supervised, temporary safe haven for children who face an emergency such as being bullied, followed, or hurt while walking or playing in the neighborhood.

See if there are any after school programs for teens and children sponsored by schools, recreation departments, churches, or community organizations like the Boys and Girls Clubs or YMCA/YWCA.

Organized patrols are another way of increasing child safety in the neighborhood. Patrollers keep an eye out for trouble, record descriptions of strangers and their cars, observe potential traffic and other hazards, and report all suspicious activity to the police or sheriff and their neighbors. This is done during the hours children travel to and from school.

Parent Alert is a program designed to inform parents if something happens to a child on the way to school. Parents often don't know until later in the day. Time is lost to law enforcement investigators when crimes are reported to them several hours after they occur.

Child abduction

Nothing is more chilling than <u>hearing</u> about a child abduction. Then we <u>saw</u> one caught on tape. The abduction of Carly Brucia gave experts an inside view of exactly how it happens and how easy it can be if children don't know what to do. As parents and educators, there are many things we can teach children to help them protect themselves. There are also many things parents can do to keep their children out of harm's way.

Start by engaging children in an open dialogue. Let children know they can tell you about any situation. There is no perfect age to teach children about personal safety. However, it is important not to scare young children. Explain to them that talking about prevention techniques and role-playing will actually make them safer. The more they know, the better they can protect themselves.

In the case of Carly Brucia, experts say she did just the opposite of what educators try to teach children. When a man approached her, she simply lowered her head and tried to walk past the man. Children should be taught to run from danger, not toward it. They also need to scream and make as much noise as possible. However, simply screaming is not good enough because all children scream when they play. Bystanders might also think the child is just throwing a temper tantrum. Teach them to yell something like "Help, I'm being kidnapped," or "Help, this is not my dad." That alone may be enough for the kidnapper to let go. The last thing a child abductor wants is for a child to make a scene and cause them to be noticed.

However, if screaming is not enough, children should do everything possible to try to get away. Teach them techniques to fight back. They are probably physically smaller, but there are several things children can do to get loose, such as kicking or biting. Check with a self-defense instructor to find out what else they can do.

Children should never take anything from a stranger including money, candy, or presents. The stranger is trying to earn trust so that children will go with him or her willingly. A kidnapper may also try to gain trust by making several minor contacts over a period of time by saying "hello" or referring to them by name.

Teach kids to stay away from cars. They should absolutely know who is in the car if they approach it. Adults should never ask kids for help. This includes asking for directions, asking if they can help them look for a pet, or asking them to help load something into a car. If a child is asked to help an adult, the child can say, "I'm sorry I can't help you," and then get away. Kids should know that there are times when they don't have to be polite. It is better for them to be safe than polite.

Forget about secret passwords. Children don't keep secrets and they forget things like passwords. Communicate with your child first-hand. If a friend is going to pick your child up from school, call your child yourself and tell him or her. Speak directly to your child, even if you have to leave a message for him or her to call you back. An abductor could call up with the same message posing as the child's mother or father.

Children should never give a stranger their name or address. Again, they don't have to be polite. They can just say, "I can't tell you that." Be careful about putting your child's name on clothing, backpacks, lunch boxes, and other property. This could put your child on a "first name" basis with an abductor.

Kids, even teenagers, should also have a buddy when they leave the house. As parents, you should know where your kids are all the time. Know who they are with and when they will be back. If you can afford it, get your kid a cell phone. They should always check in with you if there is a change in their plans.

It takes less than 10 seconds for a kidnapping to occur. Keep an eye on your kids at all times, even if you've loaded the groceries and your child into a car and you're simply returning the shopping cart. Either lock the door or keep an eye on the car at all times. Never leave a child in a car with the car running. Even if you lock the door, how hard would it be for a kidnapper to convince the child to unlock the door, especially if he or she had a handful of candy?

Children who stay home alone need special instruction on safety procedures. If the child is home alone after school, he or she should call you at work or call a trusted neighbor to let someone know he or she got home safely.

If someone calls, the caller should never know that the child is home alone. The child should say something like, "He can't come to the phone right now." This would be a good exercise to role-play. Try to throw your kids off-guard to see how they respond. Some kids will give in to a stranger's request because they can't think of how to say no. Role-playing will help keep them from becoming tongue-tied. They don't want to look foolish in front of strangers so they will tend to agree with the kidnapper. Role-playing can prepare them for these unexpected and uncomfortable scenarios.

What to do if your child is abducted

The first thing is to report a missing child to your local law enforcement agency immediately! Time is vitally important. Most children who are killed in child abduction cases are killed within two hours of being kidnapped. An abductor can escape at the rate of one mile per minute so you need to act fast.

Then ask the law enforcement agency to enter your child into the National Crime Information Center (NCIC) Missing Persons File.

Do not allow people into your house until law enforcement arrives to collect evidence. Give the police as much information as you have on your child including fingerprints, photographs, dental records, and all the facts and circumstances surrounding the disappearance.

Amber Alert

Law enforcement officials will most likely issue an Amber Alert if they believe your child has been adducted. The Amber Alert is a missing child response program that utilizes the resources of law enforcement and media to notify the public when children are kidnapped. It is named after Amber Hagerman, a nine-year-old, who was abducted and murdered near her home in Arlington, Texas in 1996.

An Amber Alert turns the public into instant investigators. Local radio and television stations agree to immediately interrupt their normal programming to broadcast information on child abductions. The information is also put on electronic highway signs that signal weather conditions.

Other criteria for deciding to issue an Amber Alert include: knowing the age of the child, and believing the child is under threat of serious bodily harm or death. This free service encourages participation between the media and law enforcement and sends a powerful message to would-be kidnappers. So far, the Amber Alert has been very effective in bringing children back home safely.

Megan's Law

Megan's Law is named after Megan Kanta, who was lured into the home of a previously convicted sex offender in 1994. She was raped and murdered right across the street from her home. Megan's Law authorizes public notification when dangerous sex offenders are released into the community.

States are not <u>required</u> to notify the community, but they are required to register sex offenders and make the information available. What this means is that law enforcement does not have to go out and knock on every door in a neighborhood. However, if you contact your local law enforcement agency and want to know where sex offenders are living, they must release this information.

Some states do indeed require law enforcement to actively notify community members door-to-door or through the mail. Other states don't require any kind of notification at all. Law enforcement may also notify a limited number of community members, for example, schools or childcare centers, who then notify parents. Call your local law enforcement agency to find out what your state is doing to alert parents about high-risk sex offenders. You can also go to www.megans-law.net, scroll to the bottom, and click on your state to find out what legislation has passed. There are also links to information on sex offenders listed by county.

Internet Safety

You always have choices as a parent. You can be a dictator and really lay down the law. You can be a pushover and have no limits whatsoever. Or you can establish some rules with your child's input and maybe even some enthusiasm! Every household will differ, but here are some suggestions to follow if you're interested in establishing basic guidelines regarding Internet use in your family.

Find out what each child wants to do. Have each child in the family list the activities he or she wants to do online, including:
- Research for school or business projects
- Online games
- Email
- General surfing
- Chat rooms, instant messaging
- Other

Discuss access privileges. Talk about freedom and responsibility with your children to see how well they understand these concepts. Ask for and consider their input as much as possible when arriving at your house rules. In general, older children should be given more input into defining the privileges of Internet use. Every household will be a little different. It is important for your children to hear your concerns and why you feel that way. It is also important to invite and listen to their ideas for solutions. Here are some questions to consider:
- Should certain kinds of Internet access be forbidden altogether?
- Should privileges be earned based on age or responsible behavior?
- Are there popular times of the day when family members need to go online? When do you need to be online?
- Are particular times more in demand than others?
- If your computer accesses the same line as your telephone, what challenges will this create?

Discuss hours of use. Determine times of the day going online will be permissible. Consider the length of sessions, the number of sessions per day, and how to take turns so that everybody's needs are met.

Draft a set of house rules. By this time, you will have covered a lot of topics with your children and will have a fairly good idea of what their needs are and what kind of access is warranted. Before drafting a set of house rules from scratch, look at the sample on the next page to see whether this list might serve as a model for your own situation.

Show a draft to your family members and give them another opportunity to give their input before you issue a final version. Try to incorporate any reasonable suggestions from your kids. This will continue the atmosphere of open communication essential to healthy and safe Internet use for the entire family.

Below is a set of house rules based on those presented in the video, *Internet Safety for Parents*. [Call Crime Prevention Resources for further information at 1-800-867-0016.] Using this as a starting point, discuss these rules with your spouse and children, and adapt it to your own particular circumstances.

House Rules (A Sample)

1. Mom or Dad must be nearby when you go online.
2. 30-minute time limit.
    a. Hours of use: 7 a.m. to 8 p.m.
    b. No use during mealtimes
3. Never disclose personal/family information without checking with a parent.
4. Never use your real name.
5. No meetings with online friends without Mom and Dad's permission.
6. No secret friends online.
7. In case of obscene or threatening mail, contact:
    1st – Mom and Dad
    2nd – Internet Service Provider
    3rd – Local Police Department
8. If it sounds too good to be true, it probably is. Contact the fraud hotline at 1-800-876-7060.
9. Downloaded files must be from known sources and scanned for viruses.
10. No chat rooms or instant messaging without checking with a parent first.
11. Privacy is earned by being responsible!

How to tell if your child is using drugs

Most parents who children become drug abusers never thought it could happen to their child. But think about this, what is to keep them from becoming a drug user. Even children who come from the best families have been known to experiment with drugs. Some of those seemingly harmless "experiments" lead to an addiction. How many "experiments" are we talking about? In 2003, the percentages of students who had used drugs in their lifetime are:

- 22.8 percent of eighth graders
- 41.4 percent of tenth graders
- 51.1 percent of twelfth graders

How many go on to use drugs regularly? In 2003, the percentages of students who had used drugs within the last 30 days of the study are:

- 9.7 percent of eighth graders
- 19.5 percent of tenth graders
- 24.1 percent of twelfth graders

No sign will pop up on your child's forehead saying that he or she is having a problem with drugs, but if you are alert, you can see some of the indications.

Actions

- Your child spends a lot of time in his or her room or away from home.
- The child appears withdrawn from family contact and activities.
- The child demonstrates a lack of responsibility.

Appearance

- You notice a change in your child's appearance and grooming habits.
- You notice a drastic change in dress.
- The child stops caring about the way he or she looks.
- She uses makeup more liberally.

Behavior – Look for
- Aggressive or withdrawn behavior.
- Mood swings – goes from happy to sad quickly.
- Poor grades in school, or drastic change in grades.
- Poor attendance in school.

Paraphernalia associated with drugs
- Roach clips – used to hold a marijuana joint when it is too small to hold with the fingers.
- Water pipes – used for smoking marijuana and other dope.
- Brass or glass pipes – also used to smoke certain types of dope.
- Cigarette lighters and matches. Many times burnt matches are found lying around the child's room.
- Eye drops – used to mask redness caused by smoking drugs.

Who can help
- School counselors can point you in the right direction.
- Law enforcement agencies may have community resource officers and drug prevention officers who can refer you to local agencies.
- Public health departments.
- Alcoholics Anonymous and Narcotics Anonymous have chapters in almost every city in North America. Check the white pages for a local phone number.
- Your family physician may be able to offer some solutions, or give you a referral.
- Check the yellow pages under Drug Treatment, Drug Abuse, and Drug Rehabilitation.

Financial Crime

Identity Theft

Identity theft occurs when someone steals personal information like a social security number and uses it to commit fraud or engage in other unlawful activities. The Federal Trade Commission has called identity theft the fastest growing crime in history. About 400,000 people will be victims of identity theft and bank account fraud this year. Not only can identity thieves drain your bank account, they can open phony accounts and run up debt in your name – before you even know it. The following are 10 strategies for lowering your risk of this crime.

1. **Guard personal information.**
    Use caution when disclosing personal information on the phone or Internet – especially your social security number, mother's maiden name, birth date, driver's license number, and bank and credit card account numbers. Don't give this information to any stranger, even one claiming to be from your bank.

2. **Dispose of documents properly.**
    Properly dispose of checks, account statements and other sensitive documents. Tear or shred them before placing them in the trash. Report lost or stolen checks immediately.

3. **Watch your trash.**
    Discourage "dumpster divers" by placing your garbage out the morning of pickup rather than the night before. Shred anything that shows your bank account or credit card numbers, anything that has your signature, and any junk mail with offers for credit.

4. **Make it harder for mail thieves.**
    Don't leave outgoing checks or paid bills in your mailbox. When ordering new checks, arrange to pick them up at the bank or have them delivered to you by registered mail.

5. **Pay attention to your accounts.**
    Scrutinize monthly billing statements. Immediately investigate any suspicious

charges. Report late statements to vendors and credit agencies.

6. Be careful when using credit and debit cards.

Be careful when using your ATM card, calling card, or credit cards. Shield them from view with your hand. Keep your eyes on your credit card during store and restaurant transactions.

7. Secure your passwords.

Keep a secure record of all passwords, credit card account numbers, expiration dates, and creditor telephone numbers and addresses. Memorize passwords and PIN numbers. Do not write them down or keep them in your wallet or purse.

8. Use care when purchasing over the Internet.

Before purchasing online, find out if the site has a secure server.

9. Stop the use of your social security number for ID purposes.

There are alternatives. Ask employers, schools, and agencies not to use your social security number as an identifier. If they refuse, make a photocopy of the ID, cut out the social security number with scissors, and carry the photocopy with you.

10. Check your credit report.

Order a copy of your credit report at least once a year from one of the three major credit bureaus listed below. This cost less than $15.

What to do if you think you're a victim of identity theft

If someone has stolen your identity, the Federal Trade Commission recommends that you complete an ID Theft Affidavit, which can be found on the Internet at www.consumer.gov/idtheft/. After completing the affidavit, the FTC advises you to take the following three steps:

1. Contact the fraud departments of each of the three major credit bureaus. Tell them to flag your file with a fraud alert including a statement that creditors should call you for permission before they open any new accounts in your name. Also request a copy of your credit report and check it for accuracy. Ask the

credit bureaus to remove the fraudulent information.

The three major credit bureaus are:

Credit bureau	To report fraud	Order a credit report
Equifax (www.equifax.com)	(800) 525-6285	(800) 685-1111
Experian (www.experian.com)	(888) 397-3742	(888) 397-3742
Trans Union (www.tuc.com)	(800) 680-7289	(800) 916-8800

2. Contact your creditors about accounts that have been tampered with or opened fraudulently. Ask to speak with someone in the security or fraud department, and follow up in writing. Following up with a letter is one of the procedures spelled out in the *Fair Credit Billing Act* for resolving errors on credit card billing statements, including charges or electronic fund transfers that you have not made.

3. File a police report with the local police where the identity theft took place. Get a copy of the report in case the bank, credit card company, or other parties need proof of the crime later on. Insist that you be given a complaint number.

Check Fraud

There are many different types of check fraud, but as a consumer you should be most concerned with check theft and check information theft. Your checks could be stolen and then used with a forged signature. Or, they could be duplicated using your checking account information to create counterfeit checks. There are many precautions you can take to prevent your checks and checking account information from being stolen.

Begin by making sure any checks you order are manufactured with security features to guard against counterfeiting and alteration to the checks. For example, some checks are made so that it is obvious if someone tries to erase a signature on a check.

When your checks arrive in the mail, verify that you received all your checks.

If it seems like your checks are taking too long to arrive, follow up to find out what happened to your order. They could have been stolen from your mailbox. Similarly, if your home is burglarized, check your checks to make sure none have been stolen. Look at all the checks. Some thieves will steal just a couple from the middle of the book or from the back. Never leave your checkbook visible in a vehicle.

Store your checks, deposit slips, bank statements, and cancelled checks in a securely locked location. Reconcile your bank statement within 30 days. You may be liable for any losses after 30 days.

When you use a check at a store, never provide more identification than necessary. A merchant should never ask for your social security number on a check. If they insist on it, take your business somewhere else.

Never give your checking account information to people you don't know or to people over the telephone, especially unsolicited sales calls. When using Internet sites, be sure to deal with reputable companies that display security features for protecting your information.

Never leave the payee or amount lines of a check blank. If someone steals the check, it's a free shopping spree. Never leave a check payable to cash lying around anywhere. These checks can be cashed by anyone. Don't endorse your checks until you are ready to cash or deposit them.

Mail theft

Do not mail your bills from your mailbox at night. Even putting them out in the morning and then leaving for work is an invitation to a daytime thief. Criminals will remove your check and either endorse it, chemically alter it, or counterfeit it. The safest place to mail your bills is from the post office.

If you do become a victim of mail theft, contact your local postal authority immediately. They will have you fill out Form 2016. Then call your local law enforcement agency. Some check thieves were caught when law enforcement circulated lists of stolen checks and the thief's check showed up at a local bank.

Then you need to close your account and notify creditors that your checks or bank statements were stolen. If a check payable to you (IRS refund, for example) is stolen, ask the sender to stop payment and issue you a new check.

Pick up your mail quickly. Mail thieves often strike within 15 minutes of the mail being delivered. If you are away on vacation, have a trusted neighbor pick up your mail or stop by the post office to stop your mail while you are gone.

Mailboxes

Here are a few suggestions for what you can do to secure your mail. Some people buy padlocks to put on their mailboxes. They place it inside the mailbox and then ask the postal carrier to lock the box after mail is delivered. This is not foolproof but can be effective. Keep in mind it might also draw attention to an otherwise ordinary box. Thieves might think there is something special in your box.

You can also replace a wall-mounted mailbox with a mail slot if you have door-to-door delivery. You need to check with your local post office before making any of these changes. Mail slots are not allowed in rural areas or newer neighborhoods with cluster boxes.

If you are disabled or a senior citizen you may be able to place your mailbox right next to your front door instead of having to walk to the end of your driveway. A mailbox directly under a porch light could make your mail safer.

Buy a security mailbox. Many companies sell tamper-resistant mailboxes. These mailboxes typically are locked but have a slot for the carrier to deliver mail.

Keep your mailbox visible. Cut shrubbery to eliminate hiding places.

If you are very concerned about theft, you can rent a mailbox from the post office or a business like Mailboxes, Etc.

Credit Card Fraud

Credit card fraud cost cardholders and issuers hundreds of millions of dollars each year. Suppose a thief rummages through your trash for carbon copies of credit card receipts. Or maybe a dishonest waitress copies (also called "skimming") your credit card number when you pay for your bill. Most people aren't aware of all the ways people can steal credit cards. But since identity theft is the fastest growing crime, people are becoming increasingly more vigilant. Here are some suggestions for how you can protect your credit cards.

Sign your cards as soon as they arrive. Signing your cards makes it harder for a thief to forge your signature.

Keep your eye on the card during a transaction. Restaurants are the one place where you lose sight of your card. Consequently, this is where skimming is most popular. A waiter or waitress may carry a $300 device called a "skimmer." When they take your credit card, they may run it through a skimmer, which records the card information. A skimmer can store several credit card numbers at a time. The legitimate information is then used to create fake credit cards. Keep track of your credit card as much as possible.

Make sure you secure the carbon copies until you get home. Put the carbons through a paper shredder if your entire credit card number is printed on them. Most carbons these days just have the last four digits of your credit card number.

Save your receipts (not the carbon copies) to compare them with the billing statements. Compare them as soon as you get the billing statement. Dispute any problems immediately by phone and in writing. Make a copy of your written communication. You cannot be held liable for more than $50 if there is a problem. (Visa and MasterCard recently waived this $50 fee.)

Keep a record of your account numbers, their expiration dates, and the phone number and address of each company in a locked place. If your credit card is stolen, you will want to have this information easily available to quickly report your missing card. Then, notify the three major credit bureaus.

Never lend your cards to anyone, and never leave your cards or receipts lying around. When you sign a receipt, put an X through any blank space above the total to prevent additions being added later.

Do not give your account number out over the phone unless you made the call, and you are sure the company is reputable. Also be sure the company is reputable when doing business over the Internet. The online merchant should have a statement about privacy and security and built-in security features on the site. Using a credit card on the Internet can be just as safe, if not safer, than using your card at a local store if the merchant uses encryption software.

The workplace is the number one place where credit cards are stolen. Never leave your cards unattended at work. Cars, hotels, and mailboxes are other hot spots for credit card theft.

Scams and Con Artists

Fraud and con games are some of the oldest known crimes. When thinking of the common criminal, the robber or burglar usually comes to mind. But what about the con artist, the cheat, or the guy selling miracle cures? They don't break into your house or use a gun, but they want your money too.

It's not only the naïve who fall victim to fraud. It can be anyone who is a little too hopeful for a miracle cure-all, a little too anxious to take advantage of a great offer, or someone who is simply unaware.

The best protection is education

Fraud takes many different forms. Some schemes involve exchanging money for worthless merchandise or property. Others offer bogus business deals and investments with the promise of high returns. Some are dishonest business practices that short-change consumers. Fraud usually takes advantage of people's desire to make money.

The best protection against fraud is to be well-informed. Immediately contact the police if you suspect fraud. It's the only way con artists can be stopped. The following are some of the most popular fraud and con games.

Home improvement fraud

Repairs and improvements on your home can be costly. Be cautious if somebody offers to do an expensive job for an unusually low price. Common hooks are:

- Offers of a "free" inspection of your home that turns up costly repairs.
- Workers "just happened to be in the neighborhood."
- Inspectors go door-to-door offering free roof, termite, or furnace inspections.
- Your house can be re-roofed at half-price because surplus materials are available from another project.
- Offers to do work on the spot.
- Offers of a price that's "too good to be true."

Who do you believe? Precautions you can take:

- Ask for and check the identification of all "inspectors."
- Always ask the firm for references – then check them! Check the contractor's reputation with the Better Business Bureau, the State

Attorney General's consumer fraud division, or county licensing agency before you authorize any work.

- Ask your friends and relatives for recommendations of other contractors.
- Get several estimates for any repair job; then compare prices and terms. Ask if there is a charge for estimates.
- Be leery of high-pressure sales tactics. "Today only" is a common ploy. Allow yourself at least 24 hours to check out the offer. Insist on a written contract for the work to be performed, and make sure you fully understand it.
- Always pay by check. Do not use cash. Set up payments in installments – one-third at the start of the job, one-third when the work is close to completion, and the remainder after the job is done. Do not pay for all of the work in advance.

Land fraud

As an investment, real estate is considered one of the best. The real estate salesperson understands how anxious you are to find the right property, especially if it is for an investment or retirement home. Common fraud hooks:

- Free swimming pool
- Country club access
- Private lake
- No mention of basics like water, energy sources, and sewage disposal

Never assume that these basics are part of the purchase. Be sure you understand the terms of a contract BEFORE you sign it. Be sure that all items mentioned in the conversation are included in the contract.

Obtain a Statement of Record. Land developers offering 50 or more lots of less than 5 acres each, for sale or lease, through the mail or by interstate commerce, are required by law to file a Statement of Record with the U.S. Department of Housing and Urban Development (HUD). The Statement of Record describes almost everything you need to know about your future home:

- Legal title
- Facilities available in the area such as schools and transportation
- Availability of utilities and water

- Plans for sewage disposal
- Local regulations and development plans

Always ask to see this report before you sign anything. The developer is required to give this information. If you are unable to obtain a copy of the property report from the developer, HUD can supply it to you for a small fee. If you are planning to purchase a rental unit, find out what the going rental rate is in the neighborhood. If purchasing vacation property or a timeshare agreement for rental income or an increase in value, be careful. The increase may never materialize.

Investment schemes

There are a number of different investment frauds including:
- Invitations to invest in a promising new company. The company takes the investor's money and quietly goes out of business.
- Pyramid schemes. Money is "invested" and you solicit others to invest also. Then they solicit others, and so on – very similar to a chain letter. Initial investors might be paid a small dividend, but when the pyramid crashes (and it always does), everybody loses except the person who started the pyramid. He or she profits because the con artist skimmed the money and never invested it.
- The pyramid franchise: the investor buys a dealership for a substantial amount and recruits other distributors or sales persons. This may result in hundreds of distributors, but no one sells the merchandise. The people at the top make lots of money before the pyramid collapses, leaving individual investors without their cash.

Warning signs for this type of scam:
- Very high-pressure telephone sales tactics.
- The deal seems too good to be true.
- The emphasis of the program is on setting up dealerships rather than selling a product.
- Potential investors are discouraged from contacting other investors.
- There is no offer to "buy back" any unsold merchandise.

Bait and switch

A product is advertised at a good price. When the customer goes into the store looking for it, the salesperson talks down the item or claims to be out of it and unable to get any more for a few months. The customer is then directed to a more expensive unit.

In this fraudulent deal, the advertiser has no intention of selling the advertised item. He or she wants to sell a substitute at a higher price. The substitute is usually inferior and at an exorbitant price.

You can prevent the bait and switch scam by staying away from these "deals." If you do decide to see the item, insist on seeing the product advertised. If you choose to purchase the advertised item despite the sales pitch, insist on buying it, not something else. If you feel you are a victim of this scam, make a complaint to your local Consumer Fraud Division and the Better Business Bureau so other people won't get conned.

Unsolicited merchandise

Someone sends you a gift in the mail such as a tie, a good luck charm, or key chain. You didn't order it. They may ask for payment for the gift. They're looking for a person who feels guilty and will pay for it. If you receive unsolicited merchandise, you are under no obligation to pay for it. If the package hasn't been opened, mark it "Return to Sender." The Post Office will send it back at no charge to you.

If the sender follows up with a visit or phone call, do not let him or her convince you that you owe something. By law, the gift is yours to keep.

Mail fraud

Any use of the mail to commit fraud constitutes mail fraud and is punishable under the law. There are many different types of mail fraud; here are a few of the more common ones.

Mail order fraud. Most catalog companies are honest and stand behind their products. A few unscrupulous companies offer worthless products, medical miracles, and get-rich-quick schemes. Scrutinize any offer. If it sounds too good to be true, it probably is.

Contest scams. You receive notice that you have won a prize. But there's always a catch! For example, "All you have to do is buy an accessory to go with your prize." The accessory usually costs more than the prize. If you're really interested in the prize, shop around for similar items. You may be able to purchase one for less than the cost of the accessory.

Cash on delivery scams. A homeowner scenario might play out like this: You are asked to accept and pay for a C.O.D. package for your neighbor who is not home. The package may be unordered goods or some worthless material. A business scenario might play out like this: A telephone call is made to ensure the employer is unavailable. The package arrives and an employee makes the payment, not suspecting any wrongdoing.

The list of con games gets longer with each new generation of con artists. There are experts who can help you determine whether you've encountered a case of mail fraud. Be sure to keep all letters and envelopes, and contact your nearest Postal Inspector to report the situation.

The pigeon drop

It's one of the world's oldest scams. A stranger begins making friendly conversation with you. A second stranger comes by, who is in cahoots with the first. The third party has just found a package containing a large sum of money. The first stranger suggests calling an attorney (a phony) for advice. The so-called attorney's advice is split the money and also set up a special account to shelter the money from taxes. You are invited to be a beneficiary of this lucky find. Everybody is required to put up some "Good Faith" money. (Guess who's first?) After you hand over your share, you never see or hear from them again.

A second variation goes like this. The stranger has found a package containing rare coins. A phone number is on the package and you are told to call the owner (a phony). The owner tells you there is a reward for the rare coins and wants to meet you. The stranger has to go and requests you give him his half of the reward with your own money. When you go to collect the reward, the "owner" is nowhere to be found. You find out the coins are worthless.

The moral: Any time a stranger wants money up front or for "Good Faith," watch out! In the excitement you may feel it is all right to give it, but it isn't. Remember that you may be dealing with professional thieves who fool people.

The bank examiner

Sometimes we can be easily impressed by authority. This is a scam that works because we don't stop to question what we are told. A so-called bank official asks you to help catch a dishonest teller. All you have to do is withdraw your savings and give the money to him so he can check the serial numbers or perform an audit. If you do agree to help, you will be taken! Remember, a real bank official would NEVER ask you to withdraw your money.

Gold and silver fraud

It can be extremely dangerous to buy and sell gold and silver coins or bars. A number of burglaries and robberies have been associated with the process. Do not give your name to anyone you have not personally confirmed to be reputable, especially when dealing in liquid items like coins, stamps, and diamonds, and particularly when cash transactions are involved. Some investors will attempt to find potential buyers through classified ads. If you try this, require and check references of people who respond to your ad. Unless you are dealing with a reliable agent at an established place of business, take some of these extra precautions:
- Watch out for prices that are too good to be true. They probably are.
- Keep gold or silver stored in safe deposit boxes and inform potential buyers or sellers where it is kept.
- Beware of counterfeit coins. Many cons use silver or gold-plated lead or brass. Phony assay stamps claiming to be "official" have been used on bullion bars or chips sealed in plastic. If purchasing coins, verify the dates and authenticity. When buying bagged silver, verify quantities. Be alert for deals in which there is only partial delivery of the valuable item. Also be wary if the delivery is under unusual circumstances.

Work-at-home scams

Most people are familiar with the newspaper or Internet ad promising a great income for performing unskilled tasks at home (such as stuffing envelopes). They always sound easy, convenient, and high-paying. As with other scams, if it sounds too good to be true, it usually is. Once you have paid for supplies or a

"How To" book to help get you started, you discover there is no market for the service or product you're supposed to produce at home. There is also no way to get your money back. Rule of thumb: Thoroughly research each opportunity. If they don't give you a way to contact them prior to your sending money, it's not worth the risk.

Funeral chasers

These con artists comb the obituary pages looking for bereaved families to prey upon. Just after the death of a relative, someone delivers a product to your door and claims that your deceased relative ordered it (e.g., a leather Bible). A bill arrives for an expensive item, demanding that you make the remaining payments. Remember, you are not responsible for anyone else's purchases. If the claim is legitimate, the estate will settle it.

Phony charities

The community needs charitable people. However, these days you need to take special precautions to ensure your money is going to a reputable organization and is used for the purposes intended. You receive a phone or mail request to donate. It's a cause you support. Are you familiar with the organization? Are you certain it's the organization you're thinking of? Some organizations have names that could be confused with each other. If you said yes, then go ahead and contribute.

If you are uncertain, do further research. Ask for identification of both the charity and the solicitor. Ask for a phone number where you can call them back. Fly by night operations won't want to provide a phone number. Ask for the organization's tax identification number and check it with your state Attorney General or consumer affairs office. Satisfy yourself about the charity's purposes, how funds are used, and if contributions are tax deductible. Send no money until you are satisfied with the answers to your questions.

Miracle cures

Any medicine claiming to be a miracle cure should be thoroughly checked out before you buy it. These scams promise preventions or cures. Some may actually be harmful or fatal if they prevent you from getting sound medical treatment.

Exaggerated claims or secret ingredients are sure warning signs. Check with your family doctor before purchasing any of these "cure-alls."

Telemarketing scams

In a free market economy, where people are promoting their businesses, telephone interruptions are a fact of life both at home and at the office. Although it is difficult to completely avoid such calls, there is much you can do to limit them. Educate yourself about the tip-offs of a possible telemarketing scam:

- You are offered something free that you did not ask for or anticipate. This should always raise suspicions.
- Someone calls to verify your VISA card number because you have won a free gift.
- An executive travel club calls and claims you've won a free vacation provided your credit card is current.
- You are offered a free product or service but must pay shipping or insurance charges.
- You receive a solicitation from a company you've never heard of.
- You are asked to sign up for an introductory offer over the phone.
- You hear phrases like "Act now," "Today only," "Prepayment required," etc.

The first thing to do is hang up. Never give your credit card number out over the phone. Ask them to put you on their "Do not call" list. While this does not always work, reputable companies will make an attempt to honor your request.

Contact the Direct Marketing Association to have your name removed from future mailing lists. This will not completely eliminate your name from circulation, but it should reduce the number of calls. The DMA also offers an opt-out service for telemarketing and email advertising. Contact the DMA by mail or over the Internet at the following address:

Direct Marketing Association
Mail Preference Service
1111 19th St. NW, Suite 1100
Washington, DC 20036-3606
www.dmaconsumers.org

You can also register on the National Do Not Call list by going to www.donotcal.gov.

What to do if you are a victim of fraud

Unscrupulous marketers will keep trying to find new victims, and sometimes even smart people can get taken. Victims of fraud are often embarrassed to admit what happened or feel that law enforcement cannot help them. Many cases go unreported because of this.

Report any suspicious situations to law enforcement. Also report it, as appropriate, to the local consumer protection office, district attorney, state Attorney General, and the National Fraud Association (1-800-876-7060, www.fraud.org). A community mediation center, Chamber of Commerce, or Better Business Bureau may be able to help you resolve the complaint.

Alert your neighbors through your Community Watch group and notify your co-workers to any known con games in the area. Educate community residents about common frauds and remedies available for victims by beginning a program specifically for fraud awareness. Write a letter to the editor of the local newspaper to warn others if you've been a victim of fraud. Lobby your city or state legislators to establish a hotline that people can call to check contractors' or solicitors' credentials.

Appendix

HOME SECURITY SURVEY

Take a few minutes to follow this list of recommendations to help secure your house. By checking off each item on the list you will significantly reduce the chances that you will be one of the millions of homes that are broken into each year.

FRONT YARD

☐ Street numbers easily visible from street. Critical time can be saved by emergency vehicles when the street address of the house is clearly visible from a distance.

☐ Bushes, shrubs and trees are pruned away from windows and doors. Burglars and thieves are less likely to break into a window or door when there is a chance to be seen.

☐ Bushes, shrubs and trees are pruned to eliminate other potential hiding places. A residence offering limited potential hiding places is less attractive to a burglar.

☐ Limited or directed access to yard. A fence with gates or shrubs at the front of the yard will create a physical and mental barrier that burglars will be less likely to cross.

☐ Locks on gates, where applicable. The ease of entrance to the yard is additionally reduced by locking out potential intruders.

☐ Lighting covers the entire front of house and all hiding places. Well-lit houses are less likely to be burglarized.

Comments:

LEFT SIDE YARD

☐ Lighting adequately covers each entrance
☐ Bushes, shrubs and trees are pruned
☐ Fence is secure

BACK YARD

☐ Lighting adequately covers each entrance.
☐ Bushes, shrubs and trees are pruned
☐ Fence is secure

RIGHT SIDE YARD

☐ Lighting adequately covers each entrance
☐ Bushes, shrubs and trees are pruned
☐ Fence is secure

OUTBUILDINGS

(Detached garage, storage sheds & barns)
☐ Locks on all doors
☐ Locks on all windows
☐ Lighting on entrances

GARAGE DOOR
☐ Internal lock
☐ External lock with hasp
☐ Hinges secure

LIVING ROOM

FRONT ENTRANCE DOOR
☐ Door construction   solid core   metal clad
☐ Dead bolt with minimum 1" throw
☐ Strike plates
☐ Door jambs secure
☐ Molding tight and secure
☐ Hinge pins on inside or otherwise secure
☐ Viewer or window in door
☐ Warning sticker clearly visible
☐ For double doors, stationary door secured
WINDOWS: ☐ SLIDER ☐ DOUBLE HUNG
☐ CRANK ☐ LOUVER
☐ Security device in place (pin or lock)
Comments:

FAMILY ROOM

Door to exterior:
PATIO DOOR
☐ Anti-slide device "Charlie Bar" or dowel
☐ Anti-lift device pin or screws in track
☐ Warning sticker clearly visible
HINGED DOOR
☐ Door construction solid core metal clad
☐ Dead bolt with minimum 1" throw
☐ Strike plates
☐ Door jambs secure
☐ Molding tight and secure
☐ Hinge pins on inside or otherwise secure
☐ Viewer or window in door
☐ Warning sticker clearly visible
☐ For double doors, stationary door secured
WINDOWS:
☐ SLIDER ☐ DOUBLE HUNG ☐ CRANK
☐ LOUVER
☐ Security device in place (pin or lock)
Comments:

HOME SECURITY SURVEY

KITCHEN/UTILITY ROOM
Door to exterior:
PATIO DOOR
- ☐ Anti-slide device "Charlie Bar" or dowel
- ☐ Anti-lift device pin or screws in track
- ☐ Warning sticker clearly visible

HINGED DOOR
- ☐ Door construction solid core metal clad
- ☐ Dead bolt with minimum 1" throw
- ☐ Strike plates
- ☐ Door jambs secure
- ☐ Molding tight and secure
- ☐ Hinge pins on inside or otherwise secure
- ☐ Viewer or window in door
- ☐ Warning sticker clearly visible
- ☐ For double doors, stationary door secured

WINDOWS: ☐ SLIDER ☐ DOUBLE HUNG
☐ CRANK ☐ LOUVER
- ☐ Security device in place (pin or lock)
Comments:

BEDROOM NO. 1.
WINDOWS: ☐ SLIDER ☐ DOUBLE HUNG
☐ CRANK ☐ LOUVER
- ☐ Security device in place (pin or lock)
Comments:

BEDROOM NO. 2
WINDOWS: ☐ SLIDER ☐ DOUBLE HUNG
☐ CRANK ☐ LOUVER
- ☐ Security device in place (pin or lock)
Comments:

BEDROOM NO. 3
WINDOWS: ☐ SLIDER ☐ DOUBLE HUNG
☐ CRANK ☐ LOUVER
- ☐ Security device in place (pin or lock)
Comments:

BEDROOM NO. 4/DEN
WINDOWS: ☐ SLIDER ☐ DOUBLE HUNG
☐ CRANK ☐ LOUVER
- ☐ Security device in place (pin or lock)
Comments:

BATHROOM NO.1
WINDOWS: ☐ SLIDER ☐ DOUBLE HUNG
CRANK ☐ LOUVER
- ☐ Security device in place (pin or lock)
Comments:

BATHROOM NO.2
WINDOWS: ☐ SLIDER ☐ DOUBLE HUNG
☐ CRANK ☐ LOUVER
- ☐ Security device in place (pin or lock)
Comments:

OTHER
WINDOWS: ☐ SLIDER ☐ DOUBLE HUNG
☐ CRANK ☐ LOUVER
- ☐ Security device in place (pin or lock)
Comments:

BASEMENT
DOOR AND WINDOWS
- ☐ Security device in place (pin or lock)
Comments:

OTHER/MISCELLANEOUS

- ☐ Skylights secured
- ☐ Automatic timers for lights, radio, & TV
- ☐ Burglar alarm system
- ☐ Emergency numbers by each phone
- ☐ Grill work on high risk windows - such as a window that may be near a lock on a nearby door.
- ☐ Inventory of contents
- ☐ Safe for valuables
- ☐ Valuables marked

NOTES:_____

_____

_____

_____

_____

BLUEPRINT FOR HOME SECURITY

Use this blueprint to help secure doors, windows and other areas of your home. You can take this form down to your local hardware store, and they can help you find the right locks and locking devices to help you be safe at home.

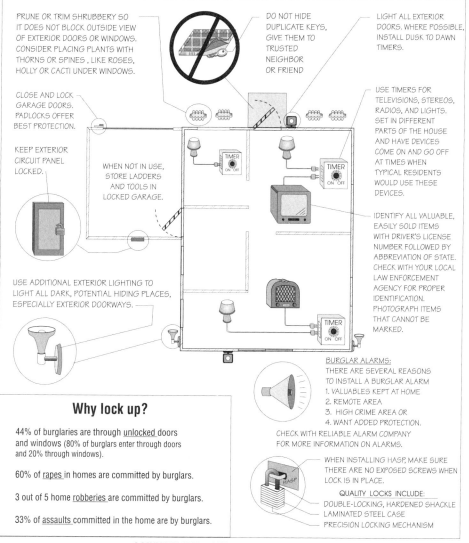

PRUNE OR TRIM SHRUBBERY SO IT DOES NOT BLOCK OUTSIDE VIEW OF EXTERIOR DOORS OR WINDOWS. CONSIDER PLACING PLANTS WITH THORNS OR SPINES, LIKE ROSES, HOLLY OR CACTI UNDER WINDOWS.

DO NOT HIDE DUPLICATE KEYS, GIVE THEM TO TRUSTED NEIGHBOR OR FRIEND

LIGHT ALL EXTERIOR DOORS. WHERE POSSIBLE, INSTALL DUSK TO DAWN TIMERS.

CLOSE AND LOCK GARAGE DOORS. PADLOCKS OFFER BEST PROTECTION.

KEEP EXTERIOR CIRCUIT PANEL LOCKED.

WHEN NOT IN USE, STORE LADDERS AND TOOLS IN LOCKED GARAGE.

USE TIMERS FOR TELEVISIONS, STEREOS, RADIOS, AND LIGHTS. SET IN DIFFERENT PARTS OF THE HOUSE AND HAVE DEVICES COME ON AND GO OFF AT TIMES WHEN TYPICAL RESIDENTS WOULD USE THESE DEVICES.

IDENTIFY ALL VALUABLE, EASILY SOLD ITEMS WITH DRIVER'S LICENSE NUMBER FOLLOWED BY ABBREVIATION OF STATE. CHECK WITH YOUR LOCAL LAW ENFORCEMENT AGENCY FOR PROPER IDENTIFICATION. PHOTOGRAPH ITEMS THAT CANNOT BE MARKED.

USE ADDITIONAL EXTERIOR LIGHTING TO LIGHT ALL DARK, POTENTIAL HIDING PLACES, ESPECIALLY EXTERIOR DOORWAYS.

TIMER ON OFF

Why lock up?

44% of burglaries are through <u>unlocked</u> doors and windows (80% of burglars enter through doors and 20% through windows).

60% of <u>rapes</u> in homes are committed by burglars.

3 out of 5 home <u>robberies</u> are committed by burglars.

33% of <u>assaults</u> committed in the home are by burglars.

BURGLAR ALARMS:
THERE ARE SEVERAL REASONS TO INSTALL A BURGLAR ALARM
1. VALUABLES KEPT AT HOME
2. REMOTE AREA
3. HIGH CRIME AREA OR
4. WANT ADDED PROTECTION.
CHECK WITH RELIABLE ALARM COMPANY FOR MORE INFORMATION ON ALARMS.

WHEN INSTALLING HASP, MAKE SURE THERE ARE NO EXPOSED SCREWS WHEN LOCK IS IN PLACE.

QUALITY LOCKS INCLUDE:
DOUBLE-LOCKING, HARDENED SHACKLE
LAMINATED STEEL CASE
PRECISION LOCKING MECHANISM

Door and Window Security

VERY IMPORTANT NOTE: WHEN SECURING DOORS AND WINDOWS, BE SURE TO ALLOW FOR FIRE ESCAPE ROUTES. BE SURE ALL FAMILY MEMBERS KNOW HOW TO UNLOCK DOORS AND WINDOWS.

HOW TO SECURE A SLIDING WINDOW

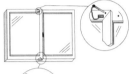

DRILL HOLE THROUGH SLIDING FRAME AND HALFWAY INTO FIXED FRAME. NOTE: DO NOT DRILL COMPLETELY THROUGH FIXED PART OF THE FRAME. (BE CAREFUL NOT TO DRILL THROUGH THE GLASS.)

USE COMMERCIAL LOCKING DEVICE WHERE PRACTICAL -- THESE LOCKS ARE ALSO AVAILABLE WITH KEYS

HOW TO SECURE A DOUBLE HUNG WINDOW

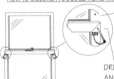

FOR VENTILATION, DRILL SECOND HOLE IN OUTSIDE SASH SO WINDOW CAN BE LOCKED OPEN. ALLOW MAXIMUM OF 3 TO 4 INCHES.

DRILL HOLE (AT DOWNWARD ANGLE) THROUGH INSIDE SASH AND 3/4" INTO OUTSIDE SASH.

USE PIN, NAIL, OR 3/16 EYE BOLT TO SECURE WINDOW

HOW TO SECURE A CRANK WINDOW

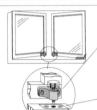

INSTALL COMMERCIAL LOCKING DEVICE ON OUTSIDE CORNER. FOR DOUBLE WINDOWS, USE A LOCKING DEVICE ON BOTH SIDES.

INSERT A METAL STRIKE PLATE IN WOODEN WINDOW SILLS.

HOW TO SECURE A LOUVER WINDOW

BECAUSE THEY ARE DIFFICULT TO SECURE, LOUVER WINDOWS SHOULD BE REPLACED. IF UNABLE TO REPLACE, USE TWO-PART EPOXY RESIN TO GLUE GLASS PANELS IN PLACE.

FOR MAXIMUM SECURITY, USE GRILLS FOR BASEMENT OR STREET LEVEL WINDOWS

HOW TO SECURE A HINGED DOOR

HINGES MOUNTED WITH PINS ON INSIDE OR USE PINS THAT CANNOT BE REMOVED

HOW TO SECURE HINGES:

REMOVE SCREW AND REPLACE WITH CUT OFF BOLT THAT PROTRUDES AT LEASE 1/4". DRILL HOLE IN OPPOSITE SIDE SO THAT WHEN THE DOOR IS CLOSED, BOLT WILL PREVENT MOVEMENT.

WARNING: This property has been marked by OPERATION ID and is recorded with law enforcement authorities.

USE ONLY HARDWOOD, SOLID-CORE OR METAL-CLAD FOR ALL EXTERIOR DOORS, INCLUDING THE DOOR TO GARAGE. A LOCK IS ONLY AS GOOD AS THE DOOR IN WHICH IT IS MOUNTED.

USE WIDE ANGLE (180 DEGREE) DOOR VIEWER (PEEPHOLE) AT EYE LEVEL.

USE STICKERS AND DECALS TO IDENTIFY YOUR HOME AS A PLACE WHERE EASY PROFITS ARE NOT FOUND. POST NEAR DOOR HANDLES AND LOCKS.

CASE HARDENED DEAD BOLT WITH 1" MINIMUM THROW ON ALL EXTERIOR DOORS.
SECURE STRIKE PLATES WITH 3" CASE HARDENED SCREWS.
MAKE SURE DOOR JAMB & MOLDINGS ARE SECURE.
WHEN MOVING IN, REKEY ALL EXTERIOR LOCKS.

HOW TO SECURE A SLIDING GLASS DOOR

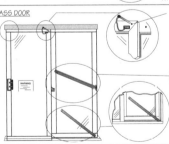

PLACE SCREWS INTO TRACK ABOVE SLIDING DOOR EVERY 8 TO 10 INCHES TO PREVENT DOOR FROM BEING LIFTED OUT OF TRACK.

DRILL HOLE THROUGH SLIDING FRAME AND HALFWAY INTO FIXED FRAME. NOTE: DO NOT DRILL COMPLETELY THROUGH FIXED PART OF THE FRAME. (BE CAREFUL NOT TO DRILL THROUGH THE GLASS.)

USE LOCKING DEVICE, ALSO CALLED "CHARLIE BAR" IN CENTER OF DOOR. VISIBLE FROM A DISTANCE, IT INFORMS POTENTIAL THIEVES YOU UNDERSTAND HOME SECURITY.

USE DOWEL STOCK OR BROOM HANDLE IN TRACK

ILLUSTRATED BY T. MONSON

HOUSEHOLD INVENTORY
Protecting the contents of your home

Why is it important to keep an accurate record of your possessions?

It is almost impossible to recreate a list of your personal possessions after a fire or burglary. You constantly collect and buy new items to add to your collection of belongings. And, in the event of a loss, it is nearly impossible to remember all that is lost.

Things like kitchen utensils, clothing, family heirlooms or antiques, valuables and other items lost in a fire or burglary may be forgotten about under the stress of loss. Years after the loss you may remember the brooch Aunt Martha gave you for your twenty-first birthday, or the fishing reel Uncle Fred gave you when you graduated from high school, but by then it is too late to claim them for your insurance or for possible tax deductions.

The only way to be sure to have an accurate record of your possessions is to create an inventory of what you have. An accurate list of everything you own is not only a good idea for fire and theft protection, but in the event you want to divide your property up in a will or present it to other family members as gifts, there will be an accurate list of your possessions.

Video taping and taking photographs add assurance that you have a complete record to quickly check to see what is missing in the event of a fire or burglary. Videos and photographs can speed up the replacement or repayment time. In the case of burglary, photographs can be used for identification -- to prove your property belongs to you, if it is recovered.

Your personal property should all be marked with your driver's license number followed by the abbreviation of the state. But this alone will not provide you with all the protection you need to ensure the replacement or recovery of what you own.

On this page and the following pages are categories and room-by-room listings for you to list your possessions and their values. Use additional sheets to list additional items and collections.

Copy these pages and when complete, store them with your important papers. Keep a copy in a safety-deposit box, with a trusted friend, or with a relative.

Items that are likely to be taken in a burglary.

ANTIQUES & HEIRLOOMS

Item /Brand /Year Purchased /Serial Number/Estimated Value /Appraised

Books
China
Clocks
Crystal
Figurines
Furniture
Lamps
Linens
Plates
Silver service
Silverware
Other

COLLECTIBLES/ART

Item /Brand /Year Purchased /Serial Number /Estimated Value /Appraised

Antiques
Art
Paintings
Figurines
Other

COLLECTIONS

Item /Brand /Year Purchased /Serial Number /Cost-Appraisal

Coins
Compact Disks
Movies
Records
Stamps
Other

CLOTHING

Item /Brand /Year Purchased /Serial Number /Cost-Appraisal

Evening Wear
Furs
Suits
Tuxedos
Other

CRAFT GOODS

Item /Brand /Year Purchased /Serial Number /Cost-Appraisal

Supplies
Tools
Other

ELECTRONICS

Item /Brand /Year Purchased /Serial Number /Cost-Appraisal

Clocks
Clock Radio
Compact Disk Player
Computer(s)
Computer Peripherals
Computer Printers
Computer Software
Games
Radios
Record Players
Stereo Equipment
Tape Recorders
Telephone
Telephone answering mach.
Televisions
Video Camera
Video Recorders
DVD Player
Records, tapes and DVDs (use separate sheet)
Other

ELECTRONIC APPLIANCES

Item /Brand /Year Purchased /Serial Number /Cost-Appraisal

Clothes Iron
Coffee Maker
Curling Irons
Fan, ceiling
Fan, portable
Hair Dryers
Microwave Oven
Sewing Machines
Toaster Ovens
Vacuum
Other

JEWELRY

Item /Brand /Year Purchased /Serial Number /Cost-Appraisal

Bracelets
Brooches
Earrings
Necklaces
Rings
Watches
Other

MUSICAL INSTRUMENTS

Item /Brand /Year Purchased /Serial Number /Cost-Appraisal

Electronic Keyboards
Organs
Piano
Other

OFFICE EQUIPMENT

Item /Brand /Year Purchased /Serial Number /Cost-Appraisal

Adding Machine
Calculator
Typewriters
Other

PHOTOGRAPHIC EQUIPMENT

Item /Brand /Year Purchased /Serial Number /Cost-Appraisal

Camera
Other

SPORTING GEAR

Item /Brand /Year Purchased /Serial Number /Cost-Appraisal

Bicycles
Bowling
Diving
Fishing
Golf
Guns
Skis
Swimming
Tennis Rackets
Other

TOOLS

Item /Brand /Year Purchased /Serial Number /Cost-Appraisal

Drills
Hand tools
Lawn mower
Power tools
Saws
Welding Equipment
Other

The following is for the recording of property items that are not necessarily prone to theft, but may be taken. You should have a record in the event of fire or some other disaster that could destroy them.

Household Items

LIVING ROOM

Number of Articles /Article /Year Purchased /Cost-Appraisal

Accessories
Air Conditioner
Books
Bookcases
Cabinets and contents
Carpet/rug
Chairs
Closet and Contents

Number of Articles /Article /Year Purchased /Cost-Appraisal

Couches
Curtains and shades
Desk
Fireplace equipment
Lamps
Tables
Wall Units
Other

DINING ROOM

Number of Articles /Article /Year Purchased /Cost-Appraisal

Accessories
Air Conditioner
Buffet
Cabinets and contents
Carpet
Chairs
Curtains and shades
Tables
Wall shelves
Other

KITCHEN, LAUNDRY ROOM

Number of Articles /Article /Year Purchased /Cost-Appraisal

Accessories
Books
Cabinets and contents
Closet and contents
Clothes Dryer
Cookers
Crockery
Cutlery

KITCHEN, LAUNDRY ROOM (CONT')

Number of Articles /Article /Year Purchased /Cost-Appraisal

Dishes
Dishwasher
Freezer
Glassware
Ironing Board
Kitchen Utensils
Linens
Pots and Pans
Refrigerator
Silverware
Stove
Tables
Washer/Dryer
Other

BEDROOM 1, MASTER

Number of Articles /Article /Year Purchased /Cost-Appraisal

Accessories
Air conditioner
Bed
Bedding
Books
Bureaus and contents
Carpets
Chairs
Chests and contents
Closet contents
Curtains and Shades
Desk
Dresser and contents
Dressing Table
Lamps
Mattresses
Springs
Tables
Wall Shelves
Other

BEDROOM 2

Number of Articles /Article /Year Purchased /Cost-Appraisal

Accessories
Air conditioner
Bed
Bedding
Books
Bureaus and contents
Carpets

BEDROOM 2 (CONT')

Number of Articles /Article /Year Purchased /Cost-Appraisal

Chairs
Chests and contents
Closet contents
Curtains and Shades
Desk
Dresser and contents
Dressing table
Lamps
Mattresses
Springs
Tables
Wall shelves
Other

BEDROOM 3

Number of Articles /Article /Year Purchased /Cost-Appraisal

Accessories
Air conditioner
Bed
Bedding
Books
Bureaus and contents
Carpets
Chairs
Chests and contents
Closet contents
Curtains and thades
Desk
Dresser and contents
Dressing table
Lamps
Mattresses
Springs
Tables
Wall shelves
Other

BEDROOM 4

Number of Articles /Article /Year Purchased /Cost-Appraisal

Accessories
Air conditioner
Bed
Bedding
Books
Bureaus and contents
Carpets
Chairs

BEDROOM 4 (CONT')

Number of Articles /Article /Year Purchased /Cost-Appraisal

Dresser and contents
Chests and contents
Closet contents
Curtains and shades
Desk
Dressing table
Lamps
Mattresses
Springs
Tables
Wall Shelves
Other

FAMILY ROOM

Number of Articles /Article /Year Purchased /Cost-Appraisal

Accessories
Air conditioners
Books
Bookcases
Cabinets and contents
Card tables
Carpet
Chairs
Closet and contents
Couches
Curtains and shades
Desk
File cabinets
Fireplace equipment
Lamps
Tables
Wall shelves
Other

HALLWAY

Number of Articles /Article /Year Purchased /Cost-Appraisal

Accessories
Cabinets and contents
Carpet
Chairs
Closet contents
Curtains and shades
Lamps
Tables
Other

BATHROOM 1,

Number of Articles /Article /Year Purchased /Cost-Appraisal

Bathroom scale

Cabinets and contents

Chairs

Clothes hamper

Linens

Other

BATHROOM 2,

Number of Articles /Article /Year Purchased /Cost-Appraisal

Bathroom scale

Cabinets and contents

Chairs

Clothes hamper

Linens

Other

BASEMENT

Number of Articles /Article /Year Purchased /Cost-Appraisal

Accessories

Carpet

Chairs

Dehumidifier

Dryer

Heating unit

Luggage

Other equipment

Rugs

Tables

Trunk and contents

Washing machines

Workbench

Other

ATTIC

Number of Articles /Article /Year Purchased /Cost-Appraisal

Furniture

Luggage

Trunk and contents

Other

GARAGE

Number of Articles /Article /Year Purchased /Cost-Appraisal

Auto equipment
Garden tools
Lawn furniture
Lawn games
Other tools
Other

ADDITIONAL LISTINGS

Item /Brand /Year Purchased /Serial Number /Cost-Appraisal

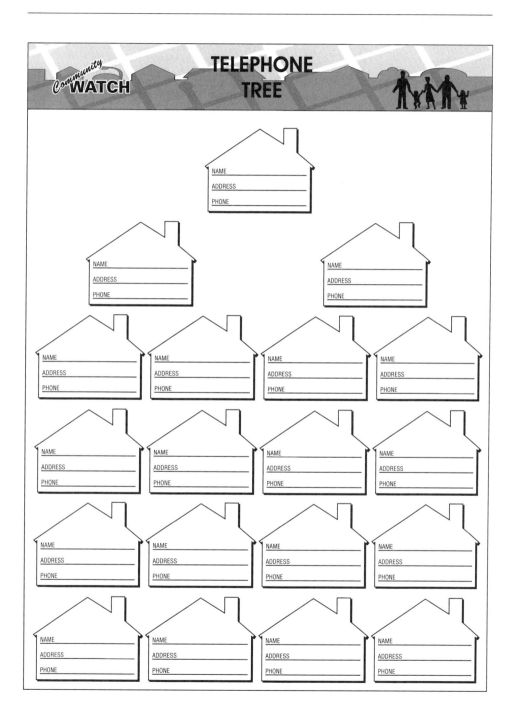

Child Identification Card

Child's name _____

Address _____

Date of birth _____

Eye color _____

Hair color_____

Weight _____ Height _____

Identifying marks _____

Native language _____

Parents' names _____

Phone numbers _____

Child's photo

Medical information

Medical conditions _____

Allergies _____

Medications _____

Blood type _____

Disabilities _____

Emergency contact _____

Emergency contact phone _____

I give medical providers permission to provide medical treatment for my child.

_____ _____
Signature   Date

Fingerprint chart

Child's name _____

Your local law enforcement agency would be happy to help you record your child's fingerprints. Or, you can get an ink pad and have your child do it him or herself with your supervision. Make sure for each print the finger is rolled gentley from left to right. Do not smudge or smear the fingerprint.

Left pinky	Left ring	Left middle	Left index	Left thumb

Right pinky	Right ring	Right middle	Right index	Right thumb